Healthy Eating in Primary Schools

Sally Robinson

P·C·P

Paul Chapman
Publishing

Paul Chapman Publishing
A SAGE Publications Company
1 Oliver's Yard
55 City Road
London EC1Y 1SP

SAGE Publications Inc.
2455 Teller Road
Thousand Oaks, California 91320

SAGE Publications India Pvt Ltd
B-42, Panchsheel Enclave
Post Box 4109
New Delhi 110 017

Commissioning Editor: George Robinson
Editorial Team: Wendy Ogden, Sarah Lynch, Mel Maines
Designer: Jess Wright

A catalogue record for this book is available from the British Library

Library of Congress Control Number 2005907007

ISBN10 1-4129-1161-3
ISBN13 978-1-4129-1161-0

Printed on paper from sustainable resources.
Printed in Great Britain by The Cromwell Press Ltd, Trowbridge, Wiltshire.

Acknowledgements

Healthy Eating in Primary Schools was inspired by the work of the Kent Healthy Schools Programme. Its development was made possible thanks to funding from the Standards Fund that supports the development of the Healthy Schools Programme in Kent, and the advice and support from the following people.

Kent Healthy Schools Programme

Liz McAvan
Jennifer Holland
Emma Harris
Hania Szczepaniak.

Consultants

Liz Twist, National Foundation for Educational Research
Professor Stephen Clift, Canterbury Christ Church University
Dr Andrew Hill, University of Leeds
Stuart McFarlane, educational consultant, Derbyshire.

Interviewees

Helen Brown
Cherie Morgan
Gill Aitken
Carmen Flynn
Carol Manton
Chris Ford
Paul Boyce
Mark Sleep
Jill Flavin
Mog Marchant
Georgina Ayin
Gillian Trumble
Sharon Bremner

Kerry Collins
Jackie Moull
Brian Molloy
Chris Beer
Fiona Annis
Carol Boxall
Liz Tanner
Paula Gill
Jennifer Holland
Carla Maurici
Camilla Joarder
Sue Scrivens
Abi Mogridge.

Piloting the lesson plans

Kirsty Vant
S. Hermitage
Ray Wookey
Pippa Holland
G. Partridge
J. Kemp
Debbie Vincent.

How to Use the CD-ROM

The CD-ROM contains PDF files, labelled 'Worksheets.pdf' which contain worksheets for each sesson in this resource. You will need Acrobat Reader version 3 or higher to view and print these pages.

The document is set up to print to A4 but you can enlarge them to A3 by increasing the output percentage at the point of printing using the page set-up settings for your printer.

Contents

Introduction

Across the UK there is a great deal of concern about the quality of children's diets and the growing problem of children's obesity. There is also anxiety about the rise of dieting and eating disorders at younger ages. Both obesity and eating disorders can be treated through educational, medical and therapeutic means with varying degrees of success. Wouldn't it be better to prevent them in the first place, or to 'nip them in the bud' before they have progressed so far as to require treatment? This is not only the message coming loudly from Government (DfES, 2004a; DoH, 2004a), but more importantly from children whose eating behaviour can be both a symptom and a cause of unhappiness (EDA, 2002; Hill and Silver, 1995; Dixey et al., 2001). *Healthy Eating in Primary Schools* shows how schools can adopt a holistic approach to promoting children's healthier eating and wellbeing.

How This Book is Structured

Chapters One to Seven: Problems and Solutions

Too many children are eating imbalanced diets which can lead to serious health problems. Today, almost a third of children are either overweight or obese (Prior et al., 2003) because many are eating too much and exercising too little. Simultaneously, dieting, eating distress and eating disorders are being seen more frequently among primary school children. Children who are very overweight or obese, those who diet or are distressed about eating, and those who have eating disorders tend to have three features in common; a fear or dislike of body fat, particular anxieties about food and the experience of very distressing emotions. Therefore in order to understand children's eating, Chapter One examines both children's diets and why they are eating these foods. Chapter Two investigates the reasons behind children's weight gain, the consequences, and some of the strategies for change. Chapter Three explores how children's bodies change and how children feel about their bodies. Chapters Four, Five and Six discuss some of the wider emotional and social factors which influence children's eating behaviour leading to dieting and eating disorders and, importantly, these chapters provide advice about what schools can do.

In order to change children into happy, healthy eaters, the food in many schools needs to be improved and the emotional and social influences on children's eating must be addressed. Children's own exploration about food, their bodies and their eating behaviour through lessons in the classroom is a vital investment in their health, and this can be enhanced by utilising the wealth of expertise in the community around the school. This holistic, multi-dimensional approach is presented within Chapter Seven.

Chapter Eight: Healthier Eating Within the Whole-school Community

Chapter 8 comprises a collection of interviews carried out with people who have each contributed towards improving the health of children in Kent. Some of the interviewees are employed by schools, and others work in the local community. They tell of introducing children to the delights of growing food, cooking food and eating healthier food, while others are helping children who have emotional concerns around food or body image. These examples provide practical ideas for schools to adopt or to adapt to their own circumstances. Each interview is complemented by useful information and resources for schools.

Chapter Nine: Lesson Plans

Chapter Nine contains 19 classroom-based lessons which can be used with junior pupils in Key Stage 2 at primary school. The lessons aim to develop children's knowledge and skills in order to help them to make decisions and feel confident in making and following through with those decisions for a healthier and happier life.

All the lessons are designed to be inclusive, meeting the needs of all children. Most are differentiated through outcome, although some include suggestions which might be more suitable for upper and lower Key Stage 2. Each lesson is linked to the *National Curriculum* (DfEE/QCA, 1999) and utilises a range of learning styles. Each lesson contributes to the skills for cognitive and affective learning which are outlined in the *Primary National Strategy, Excellence and Enjoyment: Learning and Teaching in the Primary Years* (DfES, 2004b).

The lessons begin by encouraging the children to consider why they eat what they eat, before they are introduced to the principles of a healthy diet. Each food group, within the healthy diet, is explored including the treats. The children are taken on a journey from thinking about what they eat, to what they should eat, to when and how often they should be eating in order to maintain health. Next, the children consider the importance of balancing their food intake with activity, which leads on to thinking about thinness and fatness, and body shape. Education about children's bodies is vital to counter prejudice and bullying about people's appearance and to alleviate anxiety that can lead to dieting, so the children learn about feelings and other people's feelings. The final lesson deals with food, activity, body image and feelings, a good way to bring together all of the themes that underpin healthier and happier eating.

Throughout the book, when another chapter, section or lesson is referred to, the page number follows enclosed in a circle, for example, (120)

Chapter One

Children's Eating: the Indigestible Evidence

Children's Imbalanced Diets

In 2000 the Department of Health and the Ministry of Agriculture Fisheries and Food (now DEFRA) published the results from a national survey of the diets of young people aged 4 to 18 living in Great Britain (Gregory et al., 2000).

Energy

How much energy, or calories, children need from their food is related to their age, weight, sex and physical activity. It is recommended that 7 to 10 year old boys need about 1,970 calories and girls 1,740 calories (Department of Health, 1991). If children eat more calories than they are losing through activity they gain weight.

Many children are eating more calories than they need because across the United Kingdom we are:

- eating out in restaurants and fast food outlets more than ever, and meals eaten out tend to be higher in calories and fat than those eaten at home

- snacking between meals, thus eating more, and more often

- drinking more still and carbonated sweet drinks

- eating larger portions of fast food such as 'king size' chocolate bars which can provide a fifth of the daily calories for a 10 year old.

(Department of Health, 2003)

Protein

Protein is needed for growing and repairing tissues, hence its importance for growing children. Protein from animal sources, such as meat and eggs, contain all the essential amino acids which humans need. Protein from vegetable sources, such as peas, beans and lentils, usually does not contain all the essential amino acids. This means that vegetarians need to be eating two or three vegetable sources of protein at the same meal in order to ensure that they eat all the essential amino acids.

It is recommended that 28.3 grams of protein a day will meet the needs of most 7 to 10 year olds (Department of Health, 1991). Most children are eating far more than this. In the 2000 survey boys were eating 54.8 g and girls 51.2 g, which is almost double their need. Excess protein is converted and used for energy, or it is stored as glycogen or fat in the body. This means that excess protein can contribute to children becoming overweight.

Carbohydrates

Starches and sugars are carbohydrates that are absorbed by the body. Foods high in starch include bread, pasta, rice and potatoes. Foods high in sugar include fruit, milk, chocolate and sweets. Sugar contained within fresh fruit, vegetables and milk will not damage teeth. The type of sugar that can damage teeth and gums is the non-milk extrinsic sugar. This is found in table sugar, sweets, chocolate, cakes, biscuits, fruit juice and soft drinks.

It is recommended that 50% of children's calories come from carbohydrates because they are an important source of energy (Department of Health, 1991). In the 2000 survey boys were eating 52% and girls 51% which is about right. However, it is recommended that no more than 11% of the 50% should come from carbohydrates in the form of non-milk extrinsic sugars. 89% of boys and 79% of girls were eating more than this recommended maximum.

Three-fifths of nine year olds have actively decayed or filled primary teeth (OPCS, 1994). Significant causes of decay are sugar and the high acidity associated with sweet, fizzy or alcoholic drinks and with fruit juices (Department of Health, 1989). It is because the calcium in milk helps to repair damaged tooth enamel and lower acidity in the mouth that it is recommended by the British Dental Health Foundation as a much healthier alternative drink.

Dietary fibre

Non-starch polysaccharide (NSP) is the correct name for what used to be called dietary fibre. It is a carbohydrate but unlike starches and sugars it is not absorbed by the body and therefore does not provide calories. It is thought to help in the digestion and absorption of food, and most importantly prevents constipation. Foods such as fruit, vegetables, wholegrain breakfast cereals, wholemeal bread and pasta are good sources of NSP.

There is a recommendation that the population should eat about 18 g of non-starch polysaccharide per day (Department of Health, 1991). This equates to approximately 11% of a person's daily calorie intake. There are no specific recommendations for children and 18 g might be too much for some children who shouldn't be filled with fibre at the expense of healthy nutritional food that can be absorbed. Children need as much NSP as will produce a healthy regular bowel habit and avoid constipation. Constipation is not just uncomfortable, it can lead to medical problems such as piles and diverticular disease later in life. In the 2000 survey 99% of children were eating less than 18 g of non-starch polysaccharide with 77% eating less than 10 grams. This suggests that some children are probably not eating enough NSP and could be constipated.

Fat

Fat is a concentrated source of energy. Whilst carbohydrates have approximately 3.75 calories per gram, fat contains 9 calories per gram. This is why it is so 'fattening'. Fat is an important part of children's diets because they need energy and they need some of the vitamins that are attached to fat. The chemistry of fat means that it can be saturated, unsaturated, polyunsaturated or, rarely, trans-saturated.

Saturated fats can increase blood cholesterol, leading to heart disease. As a rough guide, saturated fats are found in butter, lard, hard cheese, poultry, meat and meat products. Coconut oil is an example of an oil containing saturated fat. When looking at a food label, 5 grams of saturated fat per 100 grams of food is considered to be a lot, according to the Food Standards Agency who recommend looking for 3 grams or less.

Unsaturated (polyunsaturated or monounsaturated) fats can help to protect against heart disease. They are found in oily fish, avocados, nuts, sunflower oil, olive oil and vegetable oils. The omega 3 fatty acids, in oily fish, are particularly good for preventing clots forming in the blood, and there is some evidence that they are important for the development of the central nervous system in babies, before and after they are born. This suggests that they can influence mental development (Helland et al., 2003).

Trans fats mostly occur when vegetable oils are processed and made into margarine, and margarine is used in many biscuits, cakes and fast food. Trans fats can increase blood cholesterol. Although they should be avoided, most people eat such small quantities as to present less of a concern than saturated fats.

It is recommended that a maximum of 35% of calories should be made up of fat (Department of Health, 1991; 1994). In the 2000 survey 35% of the boys' calories came from fat, and 36% of the girls'. This means that the proportion of fat in the children's diets was about right. However, it is also recommended that no more than 11% of the fat eaten should be saturated fat. In the 2000 survey 96% of boys and 93% of the girls were eating more than this recommendation. This means that they are eating too much saturated fat, rather than the healthier polyunsaturated fats. This is likely to be a reason for studies finding high blood cholesterol in some children (Gregory et al., 2000) which is a precursor to the development of blocked arteries and heart disease.

Vitamins and minerals

Vitamins and minerals are needed in small amounts for a variety of health reasons. The reference nutrient intake (RNI) for a vitamin or mineral is the amount that is sufficient, or more than sufficient, for about 97% of a population (Department of Health, 1991). The survey in 2000 showed that primary school children were getting enough of most of the key vitamins and minerals, but they were low in zinc and girls were low in iron.

Processed and fast foods are frequently high in salt and therefore sodium. In adults there is an association between high salt intakes, age and raised blood pressure. Research is less clear about children, but there is concern that some children's consumption is too high and should be reduced to a recommended maximum of 5 grams per day (SACN, 2003). When the Food Standards Agency carried out a large survey of children's lunch boxes, they found that the average lunch box contained half the maximum daily recommended intake of salt, in addition to being high in fat and sugar (Jefferson and Cowbrough, 2004).

Fruit and vegetables

The recommendation that people should be eating approximately five portions of fruit and vegetables each day is supported by wide-ranging international (WHO, 1990) and national research (DoH 1994, 1998). This is regarded as the best protection against cancer, heart disease and stroke, other than not smoking (DoH, 2004). In a survey carried out in 2001, only 13% girls and 14% boys ate five or more portions of fruit and vegetables per day (Doyle and Hosfield, 2003). Girls ate slightly more (average 2.8 portions) than boys (average 2.6 portions). Fresh fruit is the most popular followed by fruit juices, vegetables, pulses and salad. Research has shown that adults' fruit and vegetables consumption relates to whether they have been in the habit of eating fruit and vegetables as children (Krebs-Smith, et al. 1995).

Summary of children's eating

Most children have adequate intakes of most nutrients. However, many would benefit from eating a more balanced diet.

Children in junior school are likely to be eating:

- too many calories
- too much protein, saturated fat and non-milk extrinsic sugar
- too few fruit and vegetables and too little dietary fibre.
- and/or are insufficiently physically active.

Girls in junior school are likely to be consuming too little:

- iron and zinc.

Boys in junior school are likely to be consuming too little:

- zinc.

The 2000 survey showed that after children enter secondary school the quality of many children's diets deteriorates even further.

What Children Understand by Healthy Eating

A number of research studies have investigated children's perceptions of healthy eating. Turner (1993) suggests that children between five and 12 years of age perceive vegetables, fruit, breakfast cereals, bread, cheese, fish, rice, milk, eggs, nuts and chicken to be healthy; and cakes, biscuits, sweets, crisps, chips, coke and foods high in fat such as sausages to be unhealthy. Many of these findings are supported by Lund et al.'s (1990) research with 11 year olds and Tilston et al.'s (1993) with five to eight year olds. It seems that from four years upwards children seem to develop an increasing awareness that the quality of food matters. They begin to use terms such as 'whole', 'brown' and 'fibre', and demonstrate increasing knowledge that fat, sugar and salt are unhealthy (Williams et al., 1989; Mauthner et al., 1993). Some primary school children associate fruit and vegetables with qualities such as health, slenderness, beauty and building muscles (Baranowski et al., 1993), whilst others are confused that fats and sugars cannot necessarily be seen (Tilston et al., 1993), and some children associate dietary fat more strongly with coronary heart disease than with weight gain (Dixey et al., 2001a).

However, the majority of children report that they do not care about healthy food (Mauthner et al., 1993; Watt and Sheiham, 1997; Noble et al., 2001). Baranowski et al. (1993) found that children tend to identify food that they do not like the taste of as being healthy, and that which tastes nice as being unhealthy. In Ross's study (1995) primary school children expressed a marked preference for greasy foods even though they understood that they were unhealthy. Wardle and Huon (2000) presented children with identical drinks, one of which was labelled 'healthy'. The 'healthy' drink was described as less attractive to the children. Dixey et al. (2001a) talked to nine to 11 year olds who were very well aware of the concept of a balanced diet, and the attempts by adults to manipulate their diets towards healthier eating. They were also quite capable of making their own choices. Dixey et al. report that the children were not going to be, "... coerced into a healthier lifestyle"; after all adults resist coercion and rightly so (p.77). These studies suggest the concept of health itself needs to be made positive and inviting to children.

Most nutritionists agree that it is preferable to educate children about a healthy balanced diet, in preference to 'healthy or unhealthy food', and we need to strive to make the balanced diet attractive to children.

See Lesson 1

Common Reasons for Children's Imbalanced Diets

I'm not hungry

Some children do not eat because they do not feel hungry. Over a period of time, most children will eat the amount they need. However, children who are frequently fed as a reward or in order to be comforted may start to confuse these emotional states with hunger signals and become desensitised to the physical sensations of hunger. This can lead to overeating as well as imbalanced eating (Birch, 1991).

See Lesson 1

Picky eaters and food neophobia

Picky eaters are children who choose not to eat many familiar foods. Studies have shown that picky eaters eat a smaller variety of foods than others, which results in poorer quality nutrition (Falciglia et al. 2000; Gallway et al., 2003). Children who are unwilling to try new foods because they believe that they will not like them might have a personality trait which psychologists call food neophobia, literally 'a fear of food'. Like picky eaters, studies have shown that these children are at risk of having poor quality nutrition (Falciglia et al. 2000; Gallway et al. 2003).

Harris and Booth (1992) studied infants' refusal of food and their findings help to explain some of the psychological reasons why children might refuse food.

- The child was exposed to the food and experienced a negative experience such as vomiting. The food and experience might not have been actually associated, but are so in the child's mind.

- Children have an innate preference for sweetness, but other tastes are culturally determined.

A child's tastes will be as broad or as narrow as his/her exposure to foods. The more limited their exposure, the more foods could provide neophobic reactions.

- The child needs to feel in control of their own behaviour and their own hunger/satiety, which means they might strongly dislike having their behaviour controlled by others.

Dieter and Skuse (1992) identify some ways of managing picky eaters and food neophobics.

- Reward any behaviour that comes close to eating or eating something new.

- Keep meal times happy.

- Minimise social interaction before a meal so that the interaction during the meal can be appreciated.

- Very gradually move towards new or disliked foods, such as introducing thickening very slowly. The more children are exposed to food, the more their preference for it will gradually increase (Birch and Marlin, 1982).

- Don't reward, or give attention to, eating related behaviour that you might wish to discourage. Ignore uneaten food.

- Encourage the child to eat alongside good role models such as peers or teachers who enjoy a wide variety of foods.

See Lesson 1 (120)

Patterns of eating

Whiting and Lobstein (1995) suggest that common reasons for children eating too little, or being picky eaters, are too many snacks and/or soft drinks between meals which can prevent a child from feeling hungry at meal times. Once a pattern of snacks is established, some children may deliberately refuse meals in order to have a snack of their own choice later. They suggest the replacement of soft drinks with water or a very small cup of milk, but not just before a meal, and that snacks should be limited to pieces of fruit and raw vegetable sticks.

See Fruit in School (68)

See Water in School (64)

Appearance and texture of food

Whiting and Lobstein (1995) suggest that children can be put off food if there is too much piled high on a plate, if it is not identifiable because it is too mashed up or covered in gravy, if it looks colourless, or looks sloppy or lumpy. The appearance of food matters to children, and it needs to look appetising.

Sometimes children do not eat food because they dislike the texture which may be too hard/too soft (boiled potatoes), too dry with 'bits' in (rice) (Noble et al., 2001). Charles and Kerr (1988) found that children preferred sausages and burgers to roast meat because they are easier to chew, and Baranowski et al. (1993) found that it was partly the texture of cooked vegetables which deterred children from eating them.

Whiting and Lobstein (1995 p.60) provide some good tips for encouraging children to eat vegetables:

- two or three tiny heaps of different vegetables are more appetising than one large heap of one kind

- serve small sticks or chunks of raw vegetables

- hide vegetables in soups, pizza and pancakes

- involve children in the growing and preparation of vegetables.

Noble's research suggests that the attributes of crispy, crunchy and fun to eat will make food more attractive to junior school children (Noble et al., 2001).

See Cookery Club (66)

See Growing Produce (71)

See Community Gardens (74)

See Healthy School Catering (80)

Independence and peer approval

The attractions of junk food might be in the practical, psychological and social benefits it offers to children, rather than the nutritional ones. Many children perceive that their eating in the home is largely controlled by adults (Robinson, 2000). However, in the world of junk food, children may experience the pleasure of choosing and buying 'ready to eat' burgers, chips, biscuits and sweets. This has practical benefits in that junk food rarely involves the inconvenience of requiring special utensils, cookery skills, cooking appliances or table etiquette to eat it. In fact junk food is very often finger food. The attractiveness of eating food with hands may partly explain why Baranowski et al. (1993) found that some children like fruit, why Mauthner et al. (1993) found that many of the children in their study preferred packed lunches to school dinners, and why Charles and Kerr (1988) suggest that children are better disposed to eat vegetables if they are raw. Perhaps being able to eat foods quickly and easily with hands promotes feelings of personal control.

Children also take sociability into account when making food choices. In one primary school Ross (1995) observed that many children chose the same food as their friends. In another, Mauthner et al. (1993) found that where the children sat, and who with, were more important to the children than what they ate. Places where burgers and chips are sold facilitate the interaction of young people thus providing them with a social niche which they may be unable to find elsewhere.

The value of independent eating, sociability and peer approval helps to explain the popularity of junk food, and can be used just as well to promote healthier eating in a whole-school context.

See Cookery Club (66)

See Healthy Lunch Boxes (78)

See The Schools Council and the Healthy Schools Working Group (86)

See School Nutrition Action Group (84)

See Lessons 1 and 9 (120) (149)

Adult responsibility

Children themselves are well aware that adults have a great deal of control over their eating (Robinson, 2000). Whilst genetics can explain perceptions of taste, food preferences and hunger or satiety cues, patterns of eating are based on parents' knowledge, the types of food made available by parents for children and feeding practices within the home (Davison and Birch, 2001). Parents can act as positive role models in being seen to eat and enjoy a breadth of foods, although Hill (2002) cautions that over-control can be counter-productive in that it can teach children to dislike the foods which they associate with being undermined. Over-control can also teach children to ignore their biological signals about hunger or satiety. Conversely, research also highlights that children can exploit pester power to get sweet items. 68% of seven to eight year old children in one study, reported that they usually received sweet items whenever they asked adults for them (Blinkhorn et al., 2003). This means that educating and supporting adults has to be part of the solution to children's unhealthy eating.

See Healthy Eating within the Healthy Schools Programme

See The Community Paediatrician

See Lesson 1

Advertising

Parental influence over children's food, in the context of the food industry's advertising, has been likened to a 'David and Goliath' situation (McKenzie, 2003).

Children's perceptions of food seem to be influenced by a wealth of advertising which is specifically targeted at children in order to exploit their 'pester power' (Crocket and Sims, 1995; Whiting and Lobstein, 1995). This may appear on television, radio and the internet, texts, email as well as food and drink products around any supermarket. More recently the UK has seen campaigns such as Walkers Crisps' 'Books for Schools' and the use of Tweenie images on McDonalds' Happy Meals (McKenzie, 2003). Both Walkers and Cadburys tried to reward the purchase of crisps and chocolate with sports equipment, and breakfast clubs are being targeted by Burger King (House of Commons Health Committee, 2004).

Analysis of food advertising, during children's television, shows that up to 99% of the products are high in fat, sugar and/or salt (Sustain, 2001), and that there is a remarkable overlap between foods which are advertised and those which children eat (Dibb, 1993; The Food Commission 1994, House of Commons Health Committee, 2004). This might be explained by research that has shown that until seven years old most children trust adverts; it is only at around eight that they begin to become a little more critical (House of Commons Health Committee, 2004).

In recognition of the consequences of advertising high fat, sugar and salt products to children, the Co-op has recently banned the advertising of these types of food during the hours of children's television. Instead the Co-op is advertising healthy foods at these times, and hoping that the rest of the food industry will follow its lead (Co-op, 2000). This is a move welcomed by the Food Standards Agency who launched its Food Promotion Action Plan in July 2004. This involved taking action on the advertising of foods high in fat, sugar and salt includes working with schools because, like any other setting, they can overtly or unintentionally advertise healthy or less healthy approaches to eating. The Children's Food Bill, which received its second reading in the House of Commons in October 2005, seeks a ban on advertising high fat, sugar and salt foods to children.

See Lesson 1

See Healthy Eating within the Healthy Schools Programme

See School Nutrition Action Group

School food

The quality of school food affects children's overall dietary status. According to Davison and Birch (2001), studies confirm that children's overall consumption of fat, fruit and vegetables varies according to the availability of fat, fruit and vegetables within school lunches. In a British study of nine to 11 year olds, the children described school meals as insubstantial, lacking in variety, pre-packaged and 'horrible'. The children wanted to exercise choice, and were positive about fruit tuck shops (Dixey et al., 2001).

One month after the Government had launched its *Healthy Living Blueprint for Schools* (DfES, 2004a), to promote habits for healthy living particularly through exercise and diet, the Soil Association published a survey of five meals typically served in primary schools. If a child ate these meals over a school week, they would consume 40% more salt, 28% more saturated fat and 20% more sugar than what is recommended for children, while still meeting the Government's nutritional standards for school meals (Storey et al., 2005). In February 2005, the Secretary of State for Education announced the introduction of new standards for school meals in 2006.

See The County Council 75

See Healthy School Catering 80

See Fruit in School 68

Socio-economic context

Children's diets are influenced by the wider social context in which they live. Children who live in poorer socio-economic circumstances eat poorer diets because families living on lower incomes eat more of the cheap, filling foods which are easily accessible at their local shops. This means eating a diet higher in fat and sugar and lower in fruit and vegetables (Clayton and Fewell, 1998; Gregory et al., 2000; Doyle and Hosfield 2003). Children's obesity is marginally worse in more deprived areas (Prior et al. 2003), and children in the north of England have been found to have a diet containing fewer vitamins and minerals than elsewhere in the UK (Gregory et al. 2000). The primary school children who receive free school meals receive a higher proportion of their daily energy and nutrients from these meals compared to other children (Gregory et al. 2000), and The National School Fruit and Vegetable Scheme, whereby children aged four to six receive a free piece of fruit or vegetable, aims to address the lack of availability of fresh fruit in some communities (Department of Health, 2004a).

See Breakfast Clubs  58

See Fruit in School 68

See The Family Liaison Officer 89

Culture and ethnicity

Few studies have investigated how ethnicity impacts on social aspects of eating. The evidence suggests that there are far more commonalities than differences across ethnic groups (Weber Cullen et al., 2002). Former migrants to the UK appear to vary in their cause of death, compared to the rest of the population, for example there is more obesity among South Asian, Afro-Caribbean and some Irish-born adults, but their children, born in the UK, tend to adopt British dietary patterns and have similar causes of death (Landman and Cruickshank, 2001). Specific nutritional imbalances can be associated with certain dietary practices which are associated with people's beliefs, religion and culture (Chappiti et al., 2000), but these are not common among children.

See Lessons One, Seven and Ten 120 141 152

Chapter Two

Overweight and Obesity

A Weighty Problem

Around two thirds of the population of England are overweight or obese. Obesity has grown by almost 400% in the last 25 years and on present trends will soon surpass smoking as the greatest cause of premature loss of life... On some predictions, today's generation of children will be the first for over a century for whom life-expectancy falls (House of Commons Health Committee, 2004 p.3).

According to the Chief Medical Officer:

- world wide, around 58% of type 2 diabetes, 21% of heart disease and between 8% and 42% of certain cancers are attributable to excess body fat (Department of Health, 2003)

- obesity is responsible for 9000 premature deaths each year in England, and reduced life expectancy by, on average, nine years (Department of Health, 2003)

- obesity costs the economy at least £6.6 billion a year (House of Commons Health Committee, 2004).

Among children, the worrying statistics show that:

- almost a third of all children are either overweight or obese (Prior et al., 2003)

- one in six boys under 15 are obese, representing a rise of 60% in nine years (Prior et al., 2003)

- just under 17% of girls are obese representing a rise of 42% in nine years (Prior et al., 2003)

- between 1996 and 2001, the proportion of overweight children aged six to 15 rose by 7% and obese children by 3.5% (Department of Health, 2003)

- Asian children are four times more likely to be obese than white children (House of Commons Health Committee, 2004)

- fatter children are at greater risk of developing into fatter adults compared to others (Power et al. 1997; Kotani et al., 1997; Fredricks et al., 2000)

- children are presenting with the first signs of maturity-onset diabetes which has historically been associated with middle and older age (Department of Health, 2003)

- obese children of nine years old have been found to have higher blood pressure and higher blood cholesterol than other children (Wynne, 1999)

- if current figures are projected forwards by 15 years, by the year 2020 over half UK children will be obese (House of Commons Health Committee, 2004).

See The Community Paediatrician

Reasons for Children's Increasing Weight

The balance of energy

In order for weight to remain stable, energy intake in terms of food calories must equal energy output in terms of heat or exercise. Bearing in mind that genetic make up can predispose people towards obesity (Ottley, 1997), the evidence suggests that overweight and obese people must be consuming more calories, and therefore more food, than those who are not in relation to their energy output (Garrow, 1988). The excess food which is not metabolised for energy is stored as fat. The Royal College of General Practitioners suggest that food intake, in the UK population as a whole, has fallen on average by 750 kcal per day, whilst activity levels have fallen by 800 kcals. "Out of this small imbalance has come the wave of obesity" (House of Commons Health Committee, 2004).

The House of Commons Health Committee (2004) carried out an extensive investigation into the reasons for the rise of obesity and, aside from medical reasons, it focused on food and physical inactivity.

See Lessons 11 and 13 (158) (161)

Food

In addition to the factors that encourage children to eat an imbalanced diet, the Committee found that they are encouraged to eat a high calorie diet because of the rise of energy dense foods, a snacking culture, misleading labels, super-sizing and the influence of the European Common Agricultural Policy.

See Lesson 9 (149)

Energy density of food

Energy density is the relationship between a food's calories and their volume, which relates to how filling a food is. A king size Snickers bar, weighing 100 g, has more calories than a meal of sirloin steak, potatoes and broccoli weighing 400 g. However the Snickers bar is not as filling as the meal. Foods which are high in energy density, especially those high in fat, do not tell the brain to send signals telling a person that they feel full in the same way that lower energy dense foods, or meals, do. The body has evolved in a way that it recognises volume, not calorie density. So the increase in consumption of energy dense foods, particularly as snacks in addition to meals, and the increase in consumption of highly calorific soft drinks has led to weight gain.

See Lesson 9 (149)

Snacking all day long

Unlike 50 years ago, we live in an environment where it is acceptable to eat anywhere, all day long and in larger and larger quantities. A Mintel report on snacking showed that children's pocket money had risen, on average, 45% between 1997 to 2001, meaning that they are well able to afford many of the snack foods which are quite specifically targeted towards children. Vending machines contribute £10 million to school budgets each year. Seventy per cent of parents in one study wanted a ban on vending machines. When 12 schools filled their vending machines with milk, water and fruit juice, approximately 70,000 healthier drinks were bought during the trial.

See School Nutrition Action Group (84)

See Lesson 9 (149)

Misleading labels

In England, nutrition labelling is voluntary, which can be at best confusing and at worst misleading. The food industry often charges extra for healthier options that are low in fat or sugar, yet Health Which? found that there could be up to 200% in price difference for a healthy and standard version and that some healthy versions offered very little difference. Products claiming to be 70% fat free, are high fat foods, and the premium prices for 'fun size' children's food are widely condemned. Nutrition information for meals eaten outside the home, which is a growing proportion of the UK diet, is almost non-existent.

Super-sizing

'Super-sizing' is the selling of very large portions at little extra cost. The House of Commons Health

Committee reported that McDonalds' staff are trained to promote super-sizes to customers and cinemas have taken on super-sized colas, chips and pop corn. Subsequently, in March 2004, McDonalds announced that they would be withdrawing super-sized chips and fizzy drinks from their restaurants. The documentary film *Super Size Me* (2004), written and directed by Morgan Spurlock, is an interesting and informative expose of this phenomenon.

European Common Agricultural Policy

The European Common Agricultural Policy provides consumption aid for butter and high fat milk products in schools and subsidies to promote the sale of high fat milk products and wine, whilst destroying good quality fruit and vegetables to maintain prices.

Physical inactivity

The House of Commons Health Committee (2004) also concluded that the rise in obesity was being fuelled by low levels of physical activity.

Children's inactivity

The Department of Health recommends children to take one hour of moderate activity each day. Yet a fifth of boys and girls undertake less than 30 minutes of activity each day.

Schools promoting inactivity

The Government's target that each child should undertake two hours of PE every week has led to some improvements, but one in two children still do not receive this two hours of PE in the curriculum. The British Heart Foundation National Centre for Physical Activity and Health has also noted a substantial decrease in children's activity levels during break times, exacerbated by some schools providing seating in playgrounds. The old culture, of playground games and activities, is being eroded.

Transport and lifestyle

Between 1985 and 2000 the number of primary school children being driven to school increased from 22% to 39%. This is partly because a third of primary schools refuse to allow children to bring bicycles onto the premises, and partly due to concerns about children's safety along with a history of town planning favouring the car rather than the pedestrian. Television viewing, which has doubled since the 1960s, and the rise on labour saving devices, lifts and escalators have also contributed to children's lowered activity levels.

Parental awareness

In 2005 the British Medical Journal published a study investigating parents' concerns about their children's weight. A third of mothers, and over a half of fathers, described their obese children as 'about right', signifying the desensitization of overweight in British culture (Jeffrey et al., 2005).

Solutions for Children's Increasing Weight

The House of Commons Health Committee (2004) proposed a public health strategy to prevent and control the obesity epidemic. The following solutions were recommended to Government:

- Obesity must be addressed at both an individual and environmental level.
- Government departments must work together towards Public Service Agreement targets.
- A sustained public education campaign including practical food education for children and simple food labelling.

- There must be tighter controls on advertising and promotion of foods to children.

- There is a need for improvements in children's nutrition in school, away from the promotion of high-energy dense foods and better standards for school meals.

- Pricing schemes that make healthier food more affordable need to be underpinned by reformed agricultural policies.

- There needs to be funding for, and commitment to, organised recreation in schools and outside.

- A target of three hours physical activity a week for children.

- We need imaginative approaches to broadening physical activity in schools, such as the inclusion of dance and aerobics, so that activity is enjoyable for all.

- Schools need strategies to counter bullying and promote self-esteem because overweight and obese children are all too often the victims of teasing and school sport can prove to be a humiliating experience.

- Ofsted are to include physical activity criteria in school inspections.

- There should be health impact assessment of major town planning proposals to take into account physical activity, including the promotion of cycling and walking.

- A strategic framework for preventing and treating obesity within the NHS including enabling children to have access to appropriate health services and screening for overweight and obesity within school settings.

See Healthy School Catering

See Cookery Club

See Kent Heartbeat Award Scheme

See The School Council and the Healthy Schools Working Group

See The School Nurse

See The Community Dietitian

See Lessons 13, 18 and 19

Assessing Overweight and Obesity in Childhood

The Royal College of Paediatrics and Child Health and the National Obesity Forum (Gibson et al., 2002) provide health professionals with guidance on the weight management of children.

Health professionals have access to British Childhood Body Mass Index charts that provide some guidance as to whether a child is overweight or obese. They should also take into account factors such as:

- personal and family obesity history

- personal and family medical history

- physical activity levels

- eating patterns

- academic progress

- related psychological factors such as self-esteem, bullying, depression, abuse.

See The School Nurse 94

See The Community Paediatrician 97

The Treatment of Overweight and Obese Children

The treatment of overweight and obesity in childhood should be tailored to the individual, within a context that recognises that parents are important role models. The Royal College of Paediatrics and Child Health and the National Obesity Forum (Gibson et al., 2002) suggest the following activities.

Suggestions for physical activity:

- any increase in activity will help
- aim for a sustainable lifestyle such as walking or cycling to school
- develop a whole family approach to an active lifestyle
- encourage active, enjoyable activities not embarrassing ones
- decrease sedentary activities such as watching TV.

Suggestions for healthier eating:

- a balanced, varied diet for the whole family
- regular meal times
- avoid snacks, or substitute for healthy snacks such as fruit
- encourage less energy dense food such as low fat alternatives
- encourage whole foods such as fruits and wholemeal bread
- eat at least five portions of fruit and vegetables per day
- drink water in preference to other drinks
- avoid added fat in cooking.

See The School Nurse 94

See The Community Paediatrician 97

See The Community Dietitian (113)

What Being Overweight or Obese Means for a Child

Sadly, fat children can be the victim of prejudice and abuse from other children (Renck Jalongo, 1999). One study found children describing fat children as ugly, stupid, mean, sloppy, lazy and dishonest (Wardle, et al., 1995). Recent research suggests that although some nine to 11 year olds accept that some children are 'naturally' fat and are more sympathetic in their views, they recognise that fatter children are more likely to be bullied than others (Dixey et al., 2001). Jane Wardle found that some teachers underestimate the IQ of overweight children (House of Commons Health Committee 2004). It is little wonder that research consistently shows that children who are overweight have lower self-esteem than others and do not want to be fat. Moreover this seems to be true for both girls and boys.

One of the dangers of the campaign to reduce obesity for medical reasons is that it helps to promote the social unacceptability of fatness in society. This could fuel children's negative feelings towards fat children, encourage unhealthy and unsafe eating in the name of dieting and could deter overweight children from joining in the very activities which might help them to lose weight (Wardle et al. 1995). This is why strategies which aim to reduce obesity and promote healthier eating must be informed by an understanding of how children feel about their changing bodies and how this relates to what they eat.

See Lessons 14, 15, 16, 17 and 18   (176)

Chapter Three

Body Image

Children's Body Shape Development Age 7 to 11

Children's weight and growth

British children have gained height and weight over the last 30 years (Freeman et al., 1995). This has led to puberty occurring at a younger age than ever, and in slightly more overweight children than underweight children (Freeman et al., 1995; Cole et al., 1995). Girls and boys go through similar patterns of growth until they are eight, thereafter the bodily changes for each sex, in terms of character and timing, are distinctly different (Malina and Bouchard, 1991).

Girls' development

Key features of girls' development include:

- having relatively wider hips compared to shoulder breadth in preparation for later childbirth
- having more subcutaneous fat, that is fat under the skin which affects appearance, than boys at all ages from infancy to 18 years
- a slight reduction in this fat at six or seven years old, and then it increases again
- rapid growth at about nine years, just before they enter puberty. This is called the adolescent growth spurt
- starting puberty at about ten years old, which is earlier than ever and probably due to improved nutrition. This coincides with an increase in body fat which is related to ensuring the body is ready for menarche (Bee, 1995)
- menarche usually occurring from 11 years old (Bee, 1995)
- gaining extra fat from about nine years old, in preparation for menarche, as part of their normal and healthy development.

Boys' development

Key features of boys' development are:

- having relatively wider shoulders compared to hips ready to bear the upper body's increased muscularity to come
- having less subcutaneous fat than girls throughout childhood and their teenage years
- experiencing a slight reduction in fat between six and seven, like girls. This fat increases again, but does not catch up with the girls
- experiencing the adolescent growth spurt followed by puberty at around 12 to 13 years
- experiencing increased fat just before puberty, like girls, but this is when they have entered secondary school.

Implications of girls' and boys' differing body shapes

Key ways in which boys and girls differ include:

- the way that fat is distributed around the body is similar for both girls and boys in childhood
- at nine both have more fat on their stomachs than limbs. With the onset of puberty both gain more fat on their stomachs
- at around nine girls will start to feel fat around their tummies, and boys will feel this at 12 to 13
- with puberty, girls will begin to experience fat on their thighs, upper arms and breasts.

This means that in the final years of primary school girls are moving towards increased fatness and the development of a rounded shape, whereas the boys have not yet begun the move towards increased muscularity and leanness which characterises their adolescence. In the final years of primary school, girls who have entered puberty have twice as much fat as boys (Sinclair, 1989).

It is not surprising that girls, to a greater extent than boys, start to demonstrate an awareness of their changing bodies in later primary school. Whether they have negative or positive views about these changes relates to what they are learning about acceptable and unacceptable body shapes around them.

See Lessons 14 and 15

Cultural Influences on Perceptions of Body Shape

Girls are experiencing a real increase in fatness within the context of a culture that promotes thinness as attractiveness, particularly for females (Garner and Garfinkel, 1980; Kilbourne, 1994; Macintyre and West, 1991). The thin models and pop stars are their idols and perhaps it is not surprising that many aspire to be thin at this time (Hill et al. 1992b, Hill and Silver, 1995; Grogan and Wainwright, 1996). However, this is not necessarily the underweight, under-nourished waif that adults might fear. When nine year old girls are asked to describe their ideal body image in detail the most common descriptions given are medium to thin (Robinson, 1999).

Boys are surrounded by a culture that promotes the idea that masculinity is associated with action and muscles (Watson, 1993; Kearney-Cooke and Steichen-Asch, 1990). Sportsmen, films and children's toys reflect the power of the highly muscled, classic 'V' shaped hero. Perhaps this helps to explain some of the reasons why nine year old boys want to increase their body size with muscle on their arms and legs, and do not want to be thin (Robinson, 1999; Hill et al., 1994). In this way culture might be influencing boys and girls, and their views about their bodies, in different ways.

As much as we live in a society where certain ideal feminine and masculine body shapes are associated with success, we live in one that is hostile to fatness (Cline, 1990). The multi-million pound dieting industry is testament to this. Children learn that to be fat is unacceptable and fat children become the victims of other children's cruelty. Defined by other children as weak, self-pitying and eating poorly (Edleman, 1982; White, 1983; Hill and Silver, 1995), it is little wonder that children do not want to be fat. In primary school, perhaps in different ways to teenagers in secondary schools, it is the fear of fatness that appears to be the most important influence on how children feel about their bodies.

See Lessons 14, 15 and 18

Children's Body Images

How children feel about their changing body shapes is compounded by their actual weight (Hill et al., 1992b; 1994) and by their perceptions of other children (Robinson, 1999). Although overweight children are the most unhappy with their bodies (Hill et al., 1992b; 1994), underweight children can be too (Hill et al., 1994). Many overweight children want to be thinner (Hill et al., 1992b; Blissett et al., 1996; Robinson, 1999), and many underweight children want to have more muscles in order to make themselves bigger (Robinson, 1999).

Most children have fairly accurate perceptions about their own body shape (Blissett et al., 1996), but some can have inaccurate perceptions about the bodies of other boys and girls (Robinson, 1999). Some feel that their own bodies are different to those of their same sex peers and, at an age when 'fitting in with your peers' is at a premium, the implications for self-confidence and self-esteem are self evident (Robinson, 1999).

See Lesson 14, 15, 18

Summary

By the middle of Key Stage 2 girls and boys are experiencing different changes in their bodies. They both have different body shapes. Whilst girls aspire to be thinner, they are getting unavoidably fatter. Whilst boys fear thinness, their muscles stubbornly wait to develop. Their own weight can influence how they feel, as can perceptions about their peers' bodies and body images in the wider society.

In the final year of primary school many girls will be experiencing their pubertal growth spurt, their first periods and related bodily changes such as pubic hair growth, increased perspiration and breast development. Some boys might be concerned that their bodies are not developing. About half of nine year olds are dissatisfied with their body image (Hill et al., 1992a; Hill et al., 1992b; Robinson, 1999). It seems that for children the avoidance of fatness is more important than the active pursuit of thinness seen amongst adolescent girls.

Chapter Four

Gender, Body Image and Eating

Most nutrition education is aimed at 'children', not 'boys and girls', yet their bodies, body images and indeed social perceptions of food and eating are gendered. A study carried out with 98 nine year old children sought to understand how girls and boys understand body image and food (Robinson, 1999). Some of the conclusions are outlined below.

Boys' Perceptions of Body image and Eating

- Many boys do not want to be fat and want increased muscularity.
- Boys know that eating unhealthy, junk food in large quantities encourages fatness.
- The taste of food seems to matter more than the nutritional content.
- Eating meat and eating it in large quantities is associated with masculinity.
- Boys have less nutrition knowledge and cookery skills than girls.
- Boys associate vegetables (excluding chips), salad and fruit with thinness.
- Boys associate vegetables, salad and fruit with dieting and femininity.
- Many boys do not want to be thin.

Boys have good reasons to eat junk food and to avoid fruit, salad and vegetables, and their perceptions of their body image might prevent them from doing so. So gender-sensitive education needs to make these foods attractive in a masculine context, perhaps linking them to competition, fitness and sport.

See Lessons 4 and 13

Girls' Perceptions of Body image and Eating

- Many girls want a thin to medium body image.
- Girls know that fruit, vegetables and salad can encourage thinness.
- Girls have better nutrition knowledge and cookery skills than boys.
- Girls know that fruit, vegetables and salad are healthy food.
- Eating fruit, vegetables and salad are associated with feminine eating styles.
- Dieting and eating smaller quantities is associated with femininity.
- Girls know that eating high fat food in large quantities encourages fatness.
- Girls associate meat with fatness.
- Girls do not want to be fat.

Girls have good reasons to eat small quantities and miss meals, to confuse unhealthy dieting with healthy eating and in particular to avoid meat. So gender-sensitive education needs to promote health rather than dieting, regular eating and the importance of meat and meat alternatives.

See Lessons 7, 11, 13 and 19

See The School Nurse

Chapter Five

Dieting

Dieting is Not for Children

Dieting and children generally don't mix. Health professionals supporting overweight and obese children do not recommend dieting. They recommend that children should maintain their weight or gain weight very slowly. Over time, as the child grows, the excess weight gradually falls away. This strategy emphasises a combination of healthy eating and the inclusion of physical activity in ways that are acceptable, and therefore sustainable, for the child. In certain cases, some specific individual or family behavioural therapy might be recommended, along with support to help with the psychological and social issues which an obese child might be experiencing (Gibson et al., 2002).

Children Who Diet

Primary school children are certainly aware of dieting, and can confuse dieting with healthy eating. Blissett et al. (1996) caution that just because children say that they are dieting does not mean that they are. However, it has been found that children who want to be thinner are significantly more likely to change their eating habits than those who do not (Blissett et al., 1996; Wardle 1991; Conner et al., 1991). Children's lack of knowledge about nutrition makes them vulnerable to fad and unsafe diets. Nine year olds describe their dieting in terms of missing meals – especially breakfast, eating 'slimming' foods and eating less at meal times (Hill and Robinson, 1991). These are the very types of behaviour that can lead to 'disinhibited' eating and bingeing (Crisp, 1988; Herman and Polivy, 1991).

Dieting is at its most dangerous when added to a cocktail of low self-esteem, a lack of self-confidence, coping with growing up, pressures around academic achievement, personal performance, problems with peer popularity, family tensions and media pressures (Dawson, 1995; Levine, 1987).

See The School Nurse (94)

See Schools' Counselling Service (92)

See Lessons 11, 16, 17 and 19 (159) (171) (175) (179)

How Does Dieting Begin?

Dawson (1995) outlines some of the reasons children start dieting. They:

- learn it from family and friends at an early age

- pick up dieting from others, it can become 'contagious' around a school

- feel a sense of satisfaction and control over one area of their lives

- are striving for a 'perfect' figure.

Adult Influences on Children's Eating

There is growing evidence that children's mothers are a particularly important influence on children's eating patterns and attitudes to food (Robinson, 2000). Women diet more than men (Gregory et al., 1990), and some mothers encourage their daughters to diet by restraining their daughter's eating (Johnson and Birch, 1994), and inadvertently encouraging their daughters to diet because they diet themselves (Hill et al., 1990). Gallway et al. (2003) carried out a study involving 192 seven year old girls. They found that girls who were defined as picky eaters or who had food neophobia ate fewer vegetables than others. The results also suggest that picky eating in girls was significantly related to their mother's behaviour: being breast-fed for less than six months perhaps because breast milk exposes babies to more flavours, mothers who reported not having time to eat healthily themselves, and mothers who did not eat many vegetables. Gallway et al. also found that the girls who were diagnosed as having food neophobia were more anxious, and had mothers who were more anxious than others. Conversely, some mothers encourage their sons to eat extra portions in a mistaken belief that they need more food than they are eating (Charles and Kerr, 1988).

Chapter Six

Eating Distress and Eating Disorders

Eating Distress

Florey (2004) suggests that the concept of normal eating is very broad. Whilst some people have one large meal a day, others have many small snacks. Most people experiment with food, try new food, go without food. Some people have cravings, and many find that their eating is affected by their mood. Eating might be defined as 'distressed' if someone continues to eat too much or too little over a period of time and, through denial or addiction, food starts to become the centre of their lives. Eating distress is not just about food or eating, it can be about disguising and coping with difficult feelings. The more severe types of eating distress are eating disorders.

Eating Disorders

Eating disorders are 'not about food, they are about feelings' (Eating Disorders Association, 2002). Watkins and Lask (2002) provide an excellent summary of eating disorders in children.

Childhood-onset anorexia nervosa

In childhood-onset anorexia nervosa, children will usually undertake one or two of the following practices:

- attempt to lose weight or avoid gaining weight
- restrict their food intake
- induce vomiting
- abuse laxatives
- exercise to excess.

Many children become dehydrated and their low levels of body fat leave them with insufficient resources to support healthy growth and development.

Most children with anorexia nervosa come from higher social classes, but cases from across the social spectrum are beginning to be more common. Approximately a quarter of children with this condition are boys. The boys tend to be concerned about their lack of muscularity, perceiving themselves to be flabby. They equate being overweight with being unhealthy whereas girls are more likely to associate overweight with being unattractive. Both girls and boys avoid eating food which is perceived as fattening or unhealthy and will usually exercise to excess.

Bulimia nervosa

Bulimia nervosa is rare among children. Children will usually exhibit episodes of overeating, which the child associates with a perceived loss of control, followed by measures to avoid the inevitable weight gain such as self-induced vomiting, laxative or diuretic abuse, exercising to excess or fasting. Children with bulimia nervosa often self harm and have a poor self image. There are no reports of this condition among boys.

Atypical Childhood-onset Eating Disorders

Atypical childhood-onset eating disorders are characterised by the absence of distorted thinking, yet the children's behaviour around food is discussed as being dysfunctional. This category of eating disorders includes food avoidance emotional disorder, selective eating, functional dysphagia and pervasive refusal syndrome.

Food avoidance emotional disorder

Typically children avoid food if they have this disorder. They have emotional disturbances around food and significant weight loss, but they do not have preoccupations with weight and shape. Many have additional physical illness and the food avoidance can be part of the emotional response to the physical illness.

Selective eating

Selective eaters eat very few different foods, usually concentrating on crisps, bread, biscuits or chips with milk or fruit juice. They strongly resist attempts to widen their food intake, and they do not have concerns about weight and shape. Selective eating is more common in boys than girls, by a ratio of 4:1.

Functional dysphagia

Children with functional dysphagia have a fear of swallowing, choking or vomiting, and so they avoid foods of a certain type or texture. Typically it is precipitated by an event that has allowed the food to become associated with something negative in the child's mind.

Pervasive refusal syndrome

Pervasive refusal syndrome is seen in a small number of children who refuse to eat, drink, walk, talk or care for themselves over a period of time. They become underweight, dehydrated and seriously ill, yet they typically refuse help.

How Do Eating Disorders Begin?

Tara Haggiag explains how her eating disorder began.

> At 5 years old I began to suffer from compulsive behaviour. This meant that I would take my socks on and off up to four or five times before I was satisfied. When walking along the pavement it was imperative that I avoided the cracks. This obsession with ordinary habits meant that I was late for everything and often my parents would leave me behind as a punishment. This early disorder was a signal that something was wrong. Psychiatrists advised my mother to ignore my 'negative behaviour' and reward the 'good behaviour'. As a result I felt rejected and loved only for the 'good' me.

> When I was 8 we visited my grandfather in Tuscany, and a chance remark deeply affected me. I shall never forget sitting on the grass and looking out at the glistening ocean as I experienced the last few moments of childhood innocence. My grandfather strolled past with my father and remarked, "Tara is a cute little girl, but when she loses her puppy fat she will be really beautiful." Presumably my grandfather meant well, but he was unaware of the power his poisonous words were to have. I was sensitive and remember desperately wanting to be perfect in every way.

> Before reaching my ninth birthday I had begun dieting. Along with a drastic reduction in my food intake were some rather unusual habits. I started drinking from a baby bottle and using a baby knife and fork... This baby syndrome was a desire to be a loveable baby again, like my brother who was one year old and loved by everyone. I was the eldest child and felt that somehow I was also the bad child...

> In school during lunch a child in my class tormented me: "Every bite of food you eat is making you fatter," he teased. Dieting fads filtered all the way down to the playground. Parents who slimmed passed a 'thin is best' message to their children, encouraged by the media. It is no coincidence that I obtained the starring role in my school play in the midst of my weight loss. The more I suffered from anorexia nervosa the more determined I became to be the best.

> Sensitive to the dynamics between my parents, I felt protective towards my mother and tried to prevent my parents from arguing. Refusing food was a way of gaining control over my life. It seemed to distance me from family pressure and made me feel independent. I ate alone,

making myself small portions of food in the kitchen... When anyone mentioned my unusual eating patterns I retaliated with hostility. As time went on my weight fell rapidly and the situation became out of control... The goal was to continue losing weight each day. If I maintained weight that was acceptable; if I lost weight I was satisfied and relieved.

... I remember my father chasing me up the stairs of our family house in a rage. I knew how to push all his red buttons at once and he was not always able to restrain himself... In my relationship with my father I never felt I had the space to be angry without attracting negative attention... My mother reacted differently... She closed up emotionally, seemingly detached and uninvolved... During this time I wrote a short poem describing the isolation I felt:

> I feel as though I'm in a box with a lid shut as tightly as can be, open and shut, open and shut, but the lid never opens for me.

Anorexia nervosa was a downhill struggle. I was convinced that the thinner I was the more loveable I would be to the rest of the world.

(Haggiag, 2000 p.3-5)

Tara's account reflects some of the multiple factors which, when working in combination, can lead to a child developing an eating disorder. These factors are sometimes referred to as the preconditions, immediate precipitators and perpetuators of a disorder (Levine, 1987; Watkins and Lask, 2002).

Preconditions

According to Watkins and Lask (2002), preconditions include:

- Biological factors such as serotonin levels, hormonal imbalances, anatomical and physiological abnormalities in the brain.

- Genetic factors.

- Psychological vulnerability manifested in a number of ways including low self-esteem, poor self image, perfectionism and an inability to express emotions such as anger. Children are often well behaved, conscientious, popular and high-achievers.

- Family factors, such as overprotective, rigid parenting, over compliance with the mother's needs and an inability for the child to become fully independent. Some research also suggests an association between mothers and children having atypical eating disorders.

- Cultural ideals, such as the promotion of thinness for girls and muscularity for boys.

Precipitators

- Dieting can precipitate eating disorders. By adolescence girls who are dieting are between five and 18 times more likely to develop an eating disorder than those who do not diet, depending on the severity of the dieting (Patton et al., 1999).

- Depression is strongly associated with child-onset anorexia nervosa (Bryant-Waugh, 2000), and by adolescence girls have been found to be six times more likely to develop an eating disorder compared to their happier peers (Patton et al., 1999).

- Low self-esteem can be a precondition, but can also be a precipitator. For example, children report that their eating disorder started as a result of one teasing remark abut the size or shape of their body, which is why it is so important to build children's self-esteem both in terms of their general self image and their body image. Using height and weight data as a classroom exercise can be insensitive and should be avoided (Dawson, 1995).

- Bullying and, in particular, teasing about being overweight can contribute to an eating disorder. Hence children need to understand the natural variations in body shape and size, and be part of a school culture that promotes a celebration of difference.

Anna Paterson's experience demonstrates the role that bullying played in the development of her eating disorder.

> From the age of three, I was mentally and sometimes physically abused by my grandmother. She treated me badly in many different ways, repeatedly telling me that I was worthless, unlovable, ugly and fat even though I was none of these... and gradually my self-esteem was destroyed... I saw my grandmother every day in an attempt to protect my mother... Quickly I learned that I could stop my grandmother from being cruel to my mother if I took all the abuse instead. I was too frightened to ever tell my parents about my grandmother's ill-treatment... so I stayed quiet. My grandmother often told me that I was a failure and said that I would never do well in school. This caused me to work even harder at my studies... I was wearing myself out... and by the age of 13, my body was no longer able to cope with all the abuse and hard work and it began to shut down.

(Paterson, 2002 p.8)

So a school culture which values emotional literacy and fosters a climate where children feel safe to share feelings has a better chance of preventing dieting, low self-esteem, bullying and teasing and, in turn, supports physical and emotional health.

Some suggestions for raising children's self-esteem include encouraging the children to:

- think about what they are good at and give themselves praise for it

- be proud of their skills and achievements

- talk to others they trust about how they are feeling

- talk about things which they might find difficult

- be good to themselves and treat themselves as special.

(adapted from the Eating Disorder Association web site at www.edauk.com)

See The School Nurse (94)

See The Family Liaison Officer (89)

See Schools' Counselling Service (92)

See Lessons 12, 15, 16, 17, 18 and 19 (161) (169) (171) (175) (176) (179)

Detecting an Eating Disorder

Tate (2000 p.326) advises teachers to look out for the, pupil who:

- wears layers of baggy clothing whatever the weather

- feels cold

- refuses to undress in front of others for Physical Education classes

- has withdrawn from friendship groups

- presents exceptionally neat work which contains no crossing out or corrections

- is persistently self critical of good work

- seems unable to accept praise and avoids eye contact

- fails to engage in oral work in the classroom

- works rather than socialises during breaks from class, especially during the lunch period.

The Educational Management of a Child with an Eating Disorder

Tate (2000) provides the following advice for schools, working with health professionals and parents/carers, wishing to support a child with an eating disorder:

- For a child who has been away receiving treatment, consider a preliminary ice-breaking visit before the child returns to school, and prepare the class. The pace of re-integration needs to match the child's ability to cope.

- Consider allocating a particular 'buddy' to provide company and support, and to prevent the child from becoming isolated. The buddy needs to be allocated to a named teacher who may arrange regular meetings with both children. The meetings could focus on the child's positive experiences and strengths.

- Avoid getting into battles about the child's eating at school. Focus on other areas of intervention. The child's weight will signify his/her calorie intake.

- Match academic and sports activities to the child's physical and psychological condition. Concentration could be poor, so avoid imposing unnecessary pressure.

- Try to make school a place where the child can be distracted from their eating and body image concerns. This means monitoring the child's curriculum.

- Advocate school as a place where the child can take a break from their worries.

- Consider encouraging the child to write their worries down in a book throughout the day. These could be read and discussed with an appropriate adult later.

- Encourage creative expression through activities such as art, drama and music.

- Acknowledge that the child's health and wellbeing needs take priority over achievement for the time being. The child's future can be decided upon when the condition is stable.

- Avoid encouraging perfectionism. Praise for perfection can inadvertently fuel the need to strive for it. Listen to a child's self criticism, and agree that you might have to disagree. It might be appropriate for a teacher to take in work as finished, even when the child would like to do more, in order for the child to tolerate imperfection.

- Actively seek the opinions of the child to encourage the child's self belief and practice of social interaction.

- Encourage collaborative working between the child and his/her peers.

- Be patient, positive and persevere.

Note that teachers who have, or have had, an eating disorder should not be given pastoral responsibility for a child with an eating disorder.

What to Do if You are Concerned about a Child's Eating

It is interesting to note that the emotional concerns of children who are overweight or obese have some features in common with children who are dieting or suffering from an eating disorder. These concerns include:

- a fear or dislike of fatness

- an obsession with food, weight and calories

- a strong association between food and emotions

- placing high value on their external appearance.

Whether a child is eating too much, too little or not at all, they need help.

You can:

- Build trust by letting the child know you are there, that you are concerned and that you are approachable.

- Emphasise health, apparent unhappiness, low performance or missing meals. Avoid 'too thin' or 'too committed to dieting', as these might be taken as a compliment.

- Aim for empathy and honesty.

- Ascertain whether the child is anxious about work and/or relationships at school.

- Listen to the child's peers. They probably know more than anyone else.

- Look at the expectations being put on the child, and try to reduce sources of stress.

- Find out how long the child spends on homework, and whether it is excessively long and at the expense of other appropriate social activities.

- Try to give the child opportunities where he/she can feel in control of situations and have choices.

- Maximise opportunities to raise self-esteem.

- Share your concerns with your line manager, parents and the school nurse.

(based on Dawson, 1995; Cristofoli et al., 1997; Levine, 1987; Tate, 2000)

To Teach or Not to Teach about Dieting?

Dawson (1995) recommends that children are taught about the horrific consequences of dieting and eating disorders in order to take away the mistaken romanticism attached to starvation, and the Eating Disorders Association has produced a resource to support teachers in secondary schools (EDA, 2002). However the Health Education Authority, before its demise in 1999, and the Food Standards Agency steadfastly focus on promoting healthier eating, almost never mentioning the word 'dieting'. O'Dea (2005) and practitioners have expressed concern that it is all too easy to inadvertently promote dieting, by virtue of it being associated with adult disapproval or giving children 'ideas', in school settings without meaning to do so.

Chapter Seven

A Whole-school Approach to Healthier Eating

Every Child Matters

From September 2005 Ofsted began to inspect all schools in relation to the five key outcomes, identified in *Every Child Matters* (H.M.Treasury, 2003), that are thought be the most important to children's health and wellbeing:

1. Being healthy. Enjoying good physical and mental health and living a healthy lifestyle.

2. Staying safe. Being protected from harm and neglect and growing up able to look after themselves.

3. Enjoying and achieving. Getting the most out of life and developing broad skills for adulthood.

4. Making a positive contribution to the community and to society and not engaging in anti-social or offending behaviour.

5. Economic wellbeing. Overcoming socio-economic disadvantages to achieve their full potential in life.

Healthy Eating in Primary Schools needs to embrace children's food and their diet, their emotions and the social context in which they live and learn.

This chapter provides an overview of the guidance provided at an international and national level, from HMI inspections and the Food Standards Agency. *Healthy Eating in Primary Schools* contributes to meeting the objectives of the *Healthy Living Blueprint for Schools* and the National Healthy Schools Programme. It is also supported by the findings of a comprehensive evaluation of relevant health education programmes in schools around this theme.

European Dietary Guidelines for Children and Young People

The World Health Organization (Europe) have drafted dietary guidelines for children and young people aged seven to 18 years (WHO, 2006).

Twelve steps to Healthy Eating for Children and Adolescents

1. Eat a nutritious diet based on a variety of foods originating mainly from plants, rather than animals.

2. Eat bread, grains, pasta, rice or potatoes several times a day.

3. Eat a variety of vegetables and fruits, preferably fresh and local, several times a day.

4. Replace fatty meat and meat products with beans, legumes, lentils, fish, poultry or lean meat.

5. Use low fat milk and dairy products (sour milk, yoghurt and cheese) that are low in both fat and salt.

6. Control fat intake (not more than 30% of daily energy) and replace most saturated fats with unsaturated vegetable oils or soft margarines.

7. Select foods that are low in sugar, and eat refined sugar sparingly, limiting the frequency of sugary drinks and sweets.

8. Choose a low-salt diet. Total salt intake should be limited to 5g per day, including the salt in bread and processed cured and preserved foods. (Salt iodization should be universal where iodine deficiency is endemic.)

9. Prepare food in a safe and hygienic way. Steam, bake, boil or microwave to help reduce the amount of added fat.

10. Children and adolescents should continue to learn about the preparation of food and cooking processes.

11. Explain to children and adolescents the benefits of breast-feeding, compared with infant formula.

12. Encourage children and adolescents to learn to enjoy physical activity. Reduce 'non-active' time spent on TV, video, computer games and surfing the internet and maintain body weight between the recommended limits by taking moderate levels of physical activity daily.

The Balance of Good Health

It is very difficult for many adults and children to remember which foods are good sources of which nutrients and, even when they have good nutritional knowledge, the foods may be too expensive or inaccessible. The good news is that nutritionists have found a very easy way of showing us how to achieve a healthy balanced diet. It is called the Balance of Good Health (Food Standards Agency 2005).

The Balance of Good Health is based on the Government's eight tips for eating well:

1. Base your meals on starchy foods.

2. Eat lots of fruit and veg.

3. Eat more fish – including a portion of oily fish each week.

4. Cut down on saturated fat and sugar.

5. Try to eat less salt – no more than 6 g a day for adults.

6. Get active and try to be a healthy weight.

7. Drink plenty of water.

8. Don't skip breakfast.

After the age of two, children should start to make a gradual transition towards these guidelines. Thereafter the Balance of Good Health applies to most people of all ages over the age of five unless they have particular medical problems and require a special therapeutic diet.

A healthy balanced diet can be broken into five food groups. These are summarised below.

Bread, other cereals and potatoes

This food group includes breakfast cereals, pasta, rice, noodles, cornmeal, beans, pulses, bread, potatoes. These foods are good sources of starchy carbohydrate, fibre (NSP), calcium, iron and B vitamins. We should eat plenty of these foods and try to eat wholemeal or high fibre versions where possible.

Fruit and vegetables

The fruit and vegetables in this food group can be fresh, frozen, tinned, dried or in the form of juice. Fruit and vegetables are good sources of vitamin C, carotenes (vitamin A), folates and fibre (NSP). We should eat plenty of these foods because they help to protect us from coronary heart disease, some cancers, some respiratory problems such as bronchitis and asthma, and obesity (fruit scheme). Children, like adults, should aim to eat at least five portions per day, and try to eat a wide variety. Note that fruits in the form of jam or marmalade are not included in this group.

What is a portion?

Sustain (the alliance for better food and farming) suggest that a portion is a handful. This means that a handful for a child will be smaller than a handful for an adult.

The Department of Health suggests the following portion sizes on their website www.5aday.nhs.uk/about/PortionSizes.aspx

- for large fruit: half a grapefruit or one slice of papaya or one large slice of pineapple

- for medium fruit: one apple, banana, pear, orange, nectarine or a sharon fruit.

- for small fruits: two or more plums, satsumas, kiwi fruit, apricots.

- for very small fruit it depends: seven strawberries, 14 cherries, 6 lychees.

- for dried fruit: one tablespoon of, for example, raisins, currants, sultanas.

- for tInned fruit: roughly the same quantity as that you'd eat of a fresh fruit, for example, two pear halves

- for juice: one medium (150 ml) glass of 100% fruit juice which only counts as one portion no matter how much you drink

- for green vegetables: two broccoli spears, 8 cauliflower florets, four heaped tablespoons of kale, spring greens or green beans.

- for cooked vegetables: three heaped tablespoons of cooked vegetables such as carrots, peas or sweetcorn.

- for salad vegetables: three sticks of celery, two inch piece of cucumber, one medium tomato, seven cherry tomatoes, one cereal bowl of mixed salad.

- for tinned and frozen vegetables: roughly the same as you would eat for a fresh portion.

Milk and dairy foods

This food group includes milk, cheese, yoghurt and fromage frais. We should be eating moderate amounts, less than the previous two food groups, and lower fat versions where possible. Milk and dairy foods are good sources of calcium, protein, vitamin B12, vitamin A and vitamin D. Note that this food group does not include butter, eggs or cream.

Meat, fish and alternatives

Meat, poultry, fish, eggs, nuts, beans and pulses are all included within this group. Note that pulses, such as baked beans, can be included in the bread, other cereals and potatoes food group or the fruit and vegetables group also. These foods are good sources of iron, protein, B vitamins (especially vitamin B12), zinc and magnesium.

Foods containing fat and foods containing sugar

The final food group contains foods that are high in fat, sugar or both. These foods should be eaten more sparingly than foods in other food groups, perhaps more as treats than regular components of the diet. Foods high in fat include margarine, butter, low fat spreads, cooking oil, crisps, chocolate, puddings, cake, ice cream, sauces and gravy. These foods contain essential fatty acids and some vitamins. However, most contain relatively high amounts of saturated fat that children need to try to reduce.

Foods high in sugar include sweets, soft drinks, jam, cake, puddings, biscuits, ice cream and pastries. Children need to try to reduce the amount of sugar in their diets and therefore should eat these foods in moderation, preferably at mealtimes in order to reduce the risk of tooth decay.

Water

The Water for Health Alliance reviewed scientific literature about the impact of water on health (Forrester, 2002), and found that the daily turnover of water in children is approximately 15% of total body weight, more than three times higher than adults, due to their larger surface area per unit of body weight. This means that they require 1.5 mls of water for each kilocalorie expended every day, which is approximately six to eight glasses per day. Dehydration is defined as a 1% or greater loss of body weight as a result of fluid loss, and early signs and symptoms include headaches, fatigue, loss of appetite, flushed skin, heat intolerance, light-headedness, dry mouth, loss of skin elasticity, burning sensation in the stomach and reduced concentrated urine. Drinking water in place of soft drinks is also thought to make a contribution to reducing obesity and type 2 diabetes in children.

See Water in School 64

See The Hydrate Project (105)

Salt

Salt is an essential part of a balanced diet but we do tend to eat too much which can cause heart problems. Much of what we consume is 'hidden' in other foods such as ready made meals and sauces. The Government now suggest that people aged 11 and over should aim to eat less than 6 g a day. As children are smaller, four to six year olds should eat less than 3 g a day and seven to ten year olds should eat less than 5 g a day. More information can be found at www.salt.gov.uk.

The Balance of Good Health Plate

The Balance of Good Health Plate shows the balance of the food groups on a plate, and can be a very good tool for educating children about which foods should be eaten in plentiful, which more moderately and which sparingly. On the CD-ROM there is a colour poster of the plate for your use.

See Lessons 2, 3, 4, 5, 6, 7, 8, 9 and 10 (123) (126) (129) (133) (137) (141) (146) (149) (153)

Good foods, bad foods?

It is important to note that The Balance of Good Health does not distinguish between healthy foods and unhealthy foods, good foods and bad foods, safe foods and unsafe foods, fattening foods and slimming foods because these descriptions are misleading. Whilst it might be helpful to emphasise the particular nutritional benefits of certain foods and to raise awareness about some nutritional drawbacks of others, children should be encouraged to understand that the balance of the diet is much more important than the qualities of individual foods. The Balance of Good Health teaches that all food can contribute to a nutritious diet, and eating a wide variety is to be encouraged and enjoyed.

Starting Early: Food and Nutrition of Young People

In 2004 Her Majesty's Inspectors and nutritionists reported on food and nutrition provision and practice in 19 infant and primary schools in the UK (DfES/FSA, 2004). They reported that effective practice was only seen in a minority of the infant and primary schools inspected.

Their conclusions were:

- Teachers need to be aware of reputable sources of accurate, current nutritional information, provided with easy access to this and encouraged to make regular use of it.

- Training needs to be available to develop confidence in practical food handling skills (Food Partnerships etc.).

- Other adults, particularly catering staff in schools, need up to date factual information, support and training to enable them, through the food they provide, to reflect and convey healthy eating messages and put them into practice.

- The involvement of children themselves in the decisions taken about food that is provided is vital if improvements are to go hand in hand with changes in behaviour.

HMI's conclusions underline the need for a whole-school approach towards healthier eating.

Food and Health Action Plan

In March 2005 the Department of Health announced:

- Nutritional standards for primary and secondary school meals are to be revised, and improved standards in place by September 2006. The standards will include specifications for processed foods, and standards for vending machines and tuck shops.

- Ofsted will inspect school meals as part of inspecting healthy eating in schools.

- A school catering qualification is to be introduced.

- An independent School Food Trust is to be set up to give independent support and advice to schools.

- Parents are to be encouraged to support schools in making changes to school meals through toolkits.

- A Framework for Governors, concerning the provision of school food, is to be introduced.

(Department of Health, 2005)

The School Fruit and Vegetable Scheme currently provides four to six year olds with a free piece of fruit or vegetable each school day.

See Healthy School Catering 80

See The County Council 75

See Fruit in Schools 68

Food in Schools Programme

www.foodinschools.org

The Government's Food in Schools programme aims to support teaching and learning about food through the national curriculum, and provides examples of good practice outside of the formal curriculum. It includes:

- Teaching about Food, which includes food within the national curriculum and information about food and nutrition related competencies.

- The Food in Schools Toolkit provides guidance about healthy eating throughout the school day. It includes healthier breakfast clubs, healthier tuck shops, healthier vending machines, healthier lunchboxes, the dining room environment, healthier cookery clubs, growing clubs and water provision.

- Policies and reports, which refer the reader to recent and relevant publications such as *Every Child Matters*, *Food and Health Action Plan*, *Characteristics of Good Practice in Food Technology*, and *The Chips are Down*. A useful publication is *Establishing a Whole-school Food Policy* (DfES, 2004c) which provides practical guidance about how to implement a whole-school food policy.

- An In Schools Support section which explains the National Healthy Schools Programme, School Fruit and Vegetable Scheme, School Nutrition Action Groups and 5 A Day.

- Details concerning the Primary Taste of Success Food Awards Scheme.

- Guidance about School Meals. In 2005 and 2006, the School Meals Review Panel revised the nutritional standards for school lunches. The consultation document, *Turning the Tables: Transforming School Food*, was published in October 2005. It recommended that school lunches should be based upon 14 nutrient-based standards and nine food-based standards. The nutrient standards relate to those recommended by the Caroline Walker Trust. Food standards could include the provision of at least two portions of fruit and vegetables per child per day. The final nutritional standards will be announced in January 2006, and will be available on the Department for Education and Skills web site (www.dfes.gov.uk).

- Details about Sustainable Food, which includes encouraging schools to use local producers, to improve choice, reduce waste and improve working conditions for catering staff.

- Guidance about Food Partnerships and Training. Of note is a useful publication *Establishing a Food Partnership between Primary and Secondary Schools* (DfES/Focus on Food, 2003) which encourages secondary food specialists to train and support primary colleagues.

See Growing, Cooking and Providing Healthier Food in Chapter Eight

See Providing Education About Healthier Eating in Chapter Eight

National Healthy Schools Programme

The British Government is aiming for every school to become a Healthy School and all Healthy Schools need to provide:

> ... a supportive environment including policies on smoking and healthy nutritious food, with time and facilities for physical activity and sport both within and beyond the curriculum; and comprehensive PSHE (Department of Health, 2004b, p.55)

Healthy Schools aim to meet the five key objectives outlined in the *Healthy Living Blueprint for Schools* (DfES, 2004a p.5):

1. To promote a school ethos and environment which encourages a healthy lifestyle.

2. To use the full capacity and flexibility of the curriculum to achieve a healthy lifestyle.

3. To ensure the food and drink available across the school day reinforces the healthy lifestyle message.

4. To provide high quality Physical Education and school sport and promote Physical Activity as part of a lifelong healthy lifestyle.

5. To promote an understanding of the full range of issues and behaviours which impact upon lifelong health.

Further resources to enable schools to meet these objectives can be found at www.teachernet.gov.uk/wholeschool/healthyliving.

The *National Healthy School Status: A Guide for Schools* (DfES/DH 2005) explains that schools need to meet the criteria of four core themes, using a whole-school approach, to satisfy the requirements for achieving national Healthy School status. The core themes are:

- personal, social and health education including sex and relationship education and drug education (including alcohol, tobacco and volatile substance abuse)

- healthy eating

- physical activity

- emotional health and wellbeing (including bullying)

All four themes are interdependent and relevant to a whole-school approach to the promotion of healthier eating in schools.

Personal, social and health education, including sex and relationship education and drug education (including alcohol, tobacco and volatile substance abuse)

Schools must demonstrate that they have met the following criteria with respect to the theme of PSHE.

PSHE provides pupils with the knowledge, understanding, skills and attitudes to make informed decisions about their lives.

A Healthy School:

- uses the PSHE framework to deliver a planned programme of PSHE, in line with DfES/QCA guidance (Ofsted self evaluation 4a, 4b, 4c, 4d, 4e).

Evidence:

– programme of study

– schemes of work, including opportunities to explore and understand feelings.

See Lesson Plans in Chapter Nine

- monitors and evaluates PSHE provision to ensure the quality of teaching and learning (Ofsted self evaluation 2b, 4a, 4b, 4c 4d, 4e).

Evidence:

– lesson observations by the school

– pupils' views

– staff views.

See Lesson Plans in Chapter Nine

See the Schools' Council and Healthy Schools Working Group 86

- assesses pupils' progress and achievement in line with QCA end of key stage statements (Ofsted self evaluation 4a, 4b, 4c, 4d, 4e).

Evidence:

– discussions with pupils and PSHE coordinator

– examples of assessment using the QCA end of Key Stage statements.

- has a named member of staff responsible for PSHE provision with status, training and appropriate senior management support within the school (Ofsted self evaluation).

Evidence:

– named SMT support within school

– school continuing professional development file referring to PSHE.

- has up-to-date policies in place – developed through wide consultation, implemented and monitored and evaluated for impact – covering Sex and Relationship Education, Drug Education and Incidents, Child Protection, and Confidentiality (Ofsted self evaluation 2a, 4a, 4b, 4c, 4d, 4e).

Evidence:

– sex and relationship education policy in place that has been approved by the governors

– drug education policy is in line with DfES guidance that has been approved by the governors

– managing drugs related incidents policy in line with DfES guidance that has been approved by the governors

– child protection policy in line with area child protection committee that has been approved by the governors

– confidentiality policy that has been approved by the governors

– pupils' views

– staff views.

● has an implemented non-smoking policy, or is working towards being smoke-free by September 2007 (Ofsted self evaluation 4a).

Evidence:

– the school is smoke-free OR there is an appropriate policy outlining the school's commitment to being smoke-free with a timeline included.

– staff, pupils and parents say the policy has been implemented.

● involves professionals from appropriate external agencies to create specialist teams to support PSHE delivery and to improve skills and knowledge, such as a school nurse, sexual health outreach workers and drug education advisers (Ofsted self-evaluation 4a).

Evidence:

– schemes of work reflect appropriate use of outside agencies

– policy or guidelines about how to use external visitors.

See the Schools' Counselling Service 92

See the School Nurse 94

See the Community Paediatrician 97

See the Community Dental Service 110

See the Community Dietitian 113

See Lesson Plans in Chapter Nine

● has arrangements in place to refer pupils to specialist services who can give professional advice on matters such as contraception, sexual health and drugs (Ofsted self-evaluation 4a, 4b).

Evidence:

– protocols for referral are in place.

● uses local data and information to inform activities and support important national priorities such as reducing teenage pregnancies, sexually transmitted infections and drug/alcohol misuse.

Evidence:

– staff can discuss how their healthy schools work is, to some extent, data-led, and how it supports national priorities.

● ensures provision of appropriate PSHE professional development opportunities for staff - such as the Certification Programmes for teachers and nurses offered by DH/DfES.

Evidence:

– school's continuing professional development file.

● has mechanisms in place to ensure all pupils' views are reflected in curriculum planning, teaching and learning and the whole school environment, including those with special educational needs and specific health conditions, as well as disaffected pupils, young carers and teenage parents (Ofsted self evaluation 2a, 2b).

Evidence:

– teaching and learning policy

– school inclusion policy

– pupils' views.

Healthy Eating

Schools must demonstrate that they have met the following criteria with respect to the theme of Healthy Eating.

Pupils have the confidence, skills and understanding to make healthy food choices. healthy and nutritious food and drink is available across the school.

A Healthy School:

● has identified a member of the SMT to oversee all aspects of food in the school.

Evidence:

– There is a named member of the senior management team and their role regarding healthy eating is known to staff.

● ensures provision of training in practical food education for staff, including diet, nutrition, food safety and hygiene.

Evidence:

– Continuing professional development file

– Staff who teach practical food education can discuss appropriate training.

See Healthy School Catering

● has a whole-school food policy - developed through wide consultation, implemented, monitored and evaluated for impact (Ofsted self evaluation 2a, 2b, 4a).

Evidence:

– policy

– parents/carers and pupils can describe their involvement.

See Healthy Eating within the Healthy Schools Programme

● involves pupils and parents in guiding food policy and practice within the school, enables them to contribute to healthy eating and acts on their feedback (Ofsted self evaluation 2a, 4a).

Evidence:

– discussion with pupils or returned questionnaires or focus group

– parents' and carers' views

– pupils' views.

See School Nutrition Action Group

See the Schools Council and Healthy Schools Working Group

● has a welcoming eating environment that encourages the positive social interaction of pupils (see Food in Schools guidance) (Ofsted self evaluation 4a, 4c).

Evidence:

– observation of the dining area whilst lunch is in progress

– discussion with staff and pupils regarding the dining environment

– discussion with catering staff.

See Healthy School Catering (80)

See Kent Heartbeat Award Scheme (82)

See School Nutrition Action Group (84)

See the Schools Council and Healthy Schools Working Group (86)

- ensures healthier food and drink options are available and promoted in breakfast clubs, at break (if established or planned), and at lunchtimes - as outlined by Food in Schools guidance) (Ofsted self evaluation 4a).

Evidence:

– observation of the range of food and drink available during the school day

– discussion with school task group.

- has meals, vending machines and tuck shop facilities that are nutritious and healthy (see Food in Schools guidance), and meet or exceed national standards, and is working towards the latest DfES guidance on improving school meals services (Ofsted self evaluation 4a).

Evidence:

– school meal contract that meets or is taking into consideration the latest DfES guidance on improving school meals

– menus for the week.

See The County Council (75)

See Healthy School Catering (80)

- monitors pupils' menus and food choices to inform policy development and provision (Ofsted self evaluation 4a).

Evidence:

– in discussion the school can clearly show how it undertakes this monitoring and how the data is used to inform policy.

- ensures that pupils have opportunities to learn about different types of food in the context of a balanced diet (using the Balance of Good Health), and how to plan, budget, prepare and cook meals. understanding the need to avoid consumption of foods high in salt, sugar, and fat and increase the consumption of fruit & vegetables (Ofsted self evaluation 4a).

Evidence:

– schemes of work in place.

See Lesson Plans in Chapter Nine

See Cookery Club (66)

See Fruit in School (68)

See Growing Produce (71)

See Community Gardens (74)

See Healthy Lunch Boxes (78)

- has easy access to free, clean and palatable drinking water, using the Food in Schools guidance (Ofsted self evaluation 4a).

Evidence:

– observation of the water provision

– pupils' views

– staff views.

See Water in School (64)

See The Hydrate Project (105)

- consults pupils about food choices throughout the school day using school councils, Healthy School task group or other representative pupil bodies (Ofsted self evaluation 2a, 4d).

Evidence:

– pupils' views

– minutes of meetings.

See School Nutrition Action Group (84)

See The Schools Council and Healthy Schools Working Group (86)

Physical Activity

Schools must demonstrate that they have met the following criteria with respect to the theme of Physical Activity.

Pupils are provided with a range of opportunities to be physically active. They understand how physical activity can help them to be more healthy, and how physical activity can improve and be a part of their everyday life.

A Healthy School:

- provides clear leadership provides clear leadership and management to develop and monitor its physical activity policy (Ofsted self evaluation).

Evidence:

– there is a named person and staff in the school know who that person is.

- has a whole school physical activity policy – developed through wide consultation, implemented, monitored and evaluated for impact (Ofsted self evaluation 2a, 2b, 4a, 4d).

Evidence:

– policy that covers the range of physical activity

– clear monitoring procedures are in place and promotion of physical activity reflects the stated policy

– pupils' views

– parents' and carers' views.

- ensures a minimum two hours of structured physical activity each week to all of its pupils in or outside the school curriculum (Ofsted self evaluation 4a).

Evidence:

– PE curriculum timetable

– the school's description of its provision

– pupils can describe activities available that add up to a minimum of two hours structured activity each week.

- provides opportunities for all pupils to participate in a broad range of extra curricular activities that promote physical activity (Ofsted self evaluation 4a).

Evidence:

– pupils and staff can describe the extra-curricular physical activity opportunities they have

– list of activities

- consults with pupils about the physical activity opportunities offered by the school, identifies barriers to participation and seeks to remove them (Ofsted self evaluation 2a, 4d).

Evidence:

– pupils say that they are consulted about the physical activities offered to them

– the school can specify the opportunities that have been introduced, influenced, adapted as a result of consultation.

- involves Schools Sports Coordinators (where available) and other community resources in provision of activities.

Evidence:

– reported attendance at School Sports Coordinators' network meetings

– clear use of School Sport and Club Links Strategy (PESSCL) materials identified through observation and with the physical activity coordinator

– pedestrian and cycle skills training available.

- encourages pupils, parents/carers and staff to walk or cycle to school under safe conditions, utilising the school travel plan (Ofsted self evaluation 4a, 4b).

Evidence:

– use has been made of the Safe Routes to School (SRTS) and School Travel Plan (STP) staff

– newsletter articles/letters aimed at increasing parental participation

– pupils can describe how they have been encouraged to walk or cycle to school

– the school can show the use it has made of STP surveys.

- gives parents/carers the opportunity to be involved in the planning and delivery of physical activity opportunities and helps them to understand the benefits of physical activity for themselves and their children (Ofsted self evaluation 2a).

Evidence:

– parents/carers say that they have been involved in discussing aspects of physical activity with the school

– the school can describe the work they have undertaken to encourage the involvement of parents/carers.

- ensures that there is appropriate training provided for those involved in providing physical activities.

Evidence:

– continuing professional development file

– staff discussion.

- encourages all staff to undertake physical activity.

Evidence:

– staff discussion.

Emotional health and wellbeing

Schools must demonstrate that they have met the following criteria with respect to the theme of Emotional health and well-being.

Promoting positive emotional health and well-being to help pupils understand and express their feelings, and build their confidence and emotional resilience and therefore their capacity to learn.

A Healthy School:

- identifies vulnerable individuals and groups and establishes appropriate strategies to support them and their families.

Evidence:

– special educational needs policy

– inclusion policy

– routes of referral

– system for indentification

– pupil tracking.

See the Family Liaison Officer

See the Schools' Counselling Service

See the School Nurse

See the Community Paediatrician (97)

- provides clear leadership to create and manage a positive environment which enhances emotional health and well-being in school – including the management of the behaviour and rewards policies (Ofsted self evaluation 4a, 4b, 4c).

Evidence:

– school self evaluation form

– school development plan

– discussion with head teacher and PSHE coordinator

– behaviour and rewards policy.

- has clear, planned curriculum opportunities for pupils to understand and explore feelings using appropriate learning and teaching styles (Ofsted self evaluation 4a).

Evidence:

– PSHE coordinator's views

– pupils describe how they learn to explore feelings

– learning and teaching policy

– schemes of work/programmes of study.

See Lesson Plans in Chapter Nine

- has a clear confidential pastoral support system in place for pupils and staff to access advice, especially at times of bereavement and other major life changes, and that this system actively works to combat stigma and discrimination (Ofsted self evaluation 4b).

Evidence:

– pupils understand the pastoral system

– identified route for referral for staff and pupils

– child protection policy

– inclusion policy

– examples of good practice in combating stigma and discrimination.

See the Schools' Counselling Service

- has explicit values underpinning positive emotional health which are reflected in practice and work to combat stigma and discrimination (Ofsted self evaluation 4b).

Evidence:

– prospectus or similar document

– observation.

- has a clear policy on bullying, which is owned, understood and implemented by the whole school community (Ofsted self evaluation 2a).

Evidence:

– policy

– pupils, parents/carers and staff know and understand the bullying policy

- provides appropriate professional training for those in a pastoral role.

Evidence:

– continuing professional development file

– discussions with staff

- provides opportunities for pupils to participate in school activities and responsibilities to build their confidence and self-esteem (Ofsted self evaluation 4b).

Evidence:

– programmes of study/ schemes of work

– celebrations

– behaviour and rewards policy

– learning and teaching policy

– pupils' views.

See Cookery Clubs (66)

See the Family Liaison Officer (89)

See the Hydrate Project (105)

See Lesson Plans in Chapter Nine

- has a clear confidentiality policy (Ofsted self evaluation 4b).

Evidence:

– policy OR separate sections in appropriate policies (ref 1.5)

– discussion with staff.

Educational Strategies: Recommendations from Research

Jennifer O'Dea (2005) reviewed the provision of school-based health education strategies for the improvement of body image and prevention of eating problems over the last 50 years. She writes:

> The role of health educators is complicated because of legitimate concerns that we must 'do no harm'... Health educators need to be careful to ensure that the implementation of programmes for the prevention of child obesity do not inadvertently create food concerns, body image issues, weight stigma, prejudice or eating disorders. Similarly, eating disorder prevention programmes must take care not to condone obesity nor to glamorise or normalise dieting or disordered eating. (p.11)

O'Dea's review led her to note the following points of interest:

- Interactive, student-centred learning activities are well received by students and produce positive results.

- The inclusion of boys in educational strategies are reported as being important by several authors.

- Several programmes report the value of education being delivered within a regular school environment.

- Education delivered by a teacher who has skills in facilitating small group discussions and interactive activities seems to be beneficial.

- Peer led sessions are potentially useful, as is the inclusion of parents in some positive way.

- Addressing issues of changes within the larger school environment is suggested by some authors.

- Education around the improvement of self-esteem seems to be strongly related to positive outcomes.

O'Dea cites the Health Promoting Schools Framework, based on addressing school curricula, ethos, policies and the school-community interface, as being potentially 'very powerful' citing 'outstanding improvement' in one school.

Chapter Eight

Healthier Eating within the Whole-school Community

The whole-school approach rests on the finding that children are much more likely to adopt healthier behaviours if the taught curriculum is supported by the same messages within the ethos and environment of the school and its local community (Denman et al., 2001; DFEE, 1999a; DfES, 2004a). In Kent, the Healthy Schools Programme Healthy Eating Group was set up to address Healthy Eating within the Healthy School Standard in 2000. It brought together a wide range of expertise, found common ground with their partner group leading Emotional Health and Wellbeing, and set out to disseminate their ideas to others.

This chapter comprises a collection of interviews carried out with people who have contributed towards healthier eating in Kent Schools (Appendix 1). They have each made a contribution in one of three ways:

- growing, cooking and providing healthier food
- providing emotional support for eating and/or body image problems
- providing education about healthier eating.

Each interview is complemented by sources of useful information. The organisations and websites are also listed alphabetically in Appendix 2.

Growing, Cooking and Providing Healthier Food

The following interviews provide practical examples of how healthy food can be made attractive, accessible and appetising to children.

Breakfast clubs

Helen Brown explains how to set up breakfast clubs and how they can meet the nutritional, emotional, social and educational needs of children.

School milk

Cherie Morgan is the 'Milk Lady' who works for the School Milk Project. She helps schools to access money for school milk and gives them plenty of practical support and advice.

Water in school

Gill Aitken discusses how children and staff need accessible water throughout the day to maximise concentration and feel well. Gill explains how she went about achieving water-for-all in her school.

Cookery club

Carmen Flynn teaches cookery to junior pupils and explains the very many fun-filled opportunities for learning that cookery provides.

Fruit in school

Carol Manton introduced fruit for all pupils in her school, and explains what works and why.

Growing produce

Chris Ford encourages children to grow food at her school, and shows how a Green Club can promote learning about nutrition alongside environmental health and social and organisational skills. Chris explains what works well and what to watch out for.

Community gardens

For schools who can't 'grow-their-own', Paul Boyce runs a community garden for people with learning disabilities. He explains how primary school children can visit community gardens across the country, learn about where their food comes from and how it is grown, whilst also engaging with people who are less able than themselves in a safe environment.

The County Council

Mark Sleep tackles the challenges of providing healthy school meals, and discusses the pros and cons of smart card systems.

Healthy lunch boxes

For those who do not eat school meals, Jill Flavin shares her great ideas for improving the contents of the lunch boxes that arrive at her school.

Healthy school catering

Mog Marchant is a catering manager providing good quality healthy food that the pupils really enjoy. Although she focuses on a secondary school in this interview, her catering for local primary schools is based on exactly the same principles with just as much success.

Kent Heartbeat Award Scheme

Georgina Ayin is a nutrition consultant who assesses catering premises for the Heartbeat Award in Kent. She explains what criteria schools need to meet in order to achieve an award.

School Nutrition Action Group

The School Nutrition Action Group (SNAG) was invented by the Health Education Trust. It consists of staff, pupils and external experts coming together to discuss and improve food in schools. SNAGs are slowly catching on around the country. There are no primary schools who have started a SNAG, but Gillian Trumble runs a very successful SNAG in her secondary school and talks about its progress.

The Schools Council and Healthy Schools Working Group

A variation of a SNAG group is to set up a sub-group of the School Council to address healthy eating in school. Sharon Bremner did this in her primary school and speaks with pride about what the group have achieved. At the time of writing, there are no primary schools in Kent that have started a SNAG.

Breakfast Clubs

Helen Brown
Breakfast Club Coordinator

Schools in areas of deprivation can apply to the Children's Fund for funding for their breakfast clubs. As a breakfast club coordinator I am funded by the Children's Fund to manage the budget, to support breakfast clubs through training and dissemination of good practice, and to advise on how breakfast clubs can be sustained once the funding finishes. I support 21 primary schools in the east Kent area, and visit their breakfast clubs in rotation.

A few months ago we ran a half-day training day for new members of staff involved in the breakfast clubs. Staff included family liaison officers, teaching assistants, learning support assistants, parents and kitchen staff. As well as discussing practical aspects of running breakfast clubs, I invited a community dietitian to talk about nutritional breakfasts and the client services manager from Kent County Council to talk about health and hygiene.

Breakfast clubs can be considered to be successful in different ways. I work with one junior school where there were a lot of children who were persistently late for school, absent and struggling. The family liaison officer and the deputy head teacher approached their parents and suggested that their child might like to come to the breakfast club. This has worked really well, because they were often parents with other smaller children who struggled to get everything together in the mornings. Now all they have to do is get the child up and dressed and to school, and then they can return home to give the smaller children breakfast. It eases the load for the parents and the child's attendance improves. The staff play games and Circle Time with the children at the breakfast club which enables the children to focus and get in the mood for learning. It is really impressive. However, this school isn't so good on the healthy eating side. They have to use the school kitchen and the school cook provides the breakfast. It wasn't a very healthy breakfast, but in other ways the social and educational aspects of the breakfast club are working well.

At one infant school there is a successful breakfast club in terms of the food being very healthy. The breakfast includes plenty of fruit and non-sugary cereals. They are encouraged not to add sugar to cereals, and it is all very attractively presented. The staff have worked with some of the obese children, encouraging healthy eating and explaining the benefits of eating fruit. They also follow up the breakfast with activities that encourage the children to focus, before they go into class.

If schools want to introduce a breakfast club into their schools, the first point of contact is usually their local Healthy Schools team based within their primary care trust. Food in Schools (www.foodinschools.org) also provides very useful information.

Useful Information

Evidence and advice for breakfast clubs

Breakfast clubs were introduced into UK schools in the 1990s because of concerns about children's imbalanced diets and the educational difficulties associated with erratic attendance and poor concentration. For children who do not otherwise obtain a balanced meal at the beginning of the day, breakfast at school can contribute to their nutritional, psychological and social wellbeing, it can improve their attendance and can help them to start their day feeling settled and safe (Donovan and Street, 1999). In *Breakfast Clubs: A How To Guide* (New Policy Institute and Kelloggs, 2000) the Government officially endorses breakfast clubs as making an important contribution towards children's health and education. However, as yet, they are not part of the Government's mainstream provision, and schools have to access external funding sources to set them up.

Breakfast Club Plus

Breakfast Club Plus is a network that supports breakfast clubs throughout the UK. The web site contains details about useful resources and ideas.

www.breakfast-club.co.uk

Cereal offenders

As part of The Consumers' Association's nutrition campaign 'Health Warning to Government' launched in 2004, it carried out a special investigation into breakfast cereals. Using guidelines from the Food Standards Agency they rated cereals in terms of fibre, salt and sugar.

Better options, of those cereals directly marketed to children included:

- Weetabix Ready Brek (original) – high fibre, low salt, low sugar
- Weetabix Ready Brek (chocolate) – high fibre, low salt, low sugar
- Quaker Sugar Puffs – moderate fibre, low salt, high sugar
- Nestle Coco Shreddies and Nestle Frosted Shreddies – high fibre, moderate salt, high sugar
- Kellogg's Coco Pops Crunchers and Weetabix Weetos – moderate fibre, moderate salt, high sugar.

Better options, of those cereals not specifically marketed to children included:

- Nestle Shredded Wheat, Nestle Shredded Wheat Bitesize, Quaker Oatso Simple (original), all types of plain porridge oats – high fibre, low salt, low sugar
- Weetabix, Weetabix Organic – low fibre, moderate salt, moderate sugar
- Jordans Luxury Crunchy (golden maple and pecan), Jordans Natural Muesli, Kellogg's Frosted Wheats, Kellogg's Raisin Wheats, Nestle Honey Nut Shredded Wheat – high fibre, low salt, high sugar
- Jordans Original Crunchy – moderate fibre, low salt, high sugar
- Jordans Nature's Wholegrain, Quaker Oatso Simple (flavoured), Weetabix Alpen, Jordans Luxury Crunch (golden honey and nut) – high fibre, moderate salt, high sugar.

Worst offenders, of cereals directly marketed to children included:

- Nestle Lion Cereal – low fibre, moderate salt, high sugar, high saturated fat, contains trans fat
- Kellogg's Frosties Turbos, Nestle Cookie Crisp – low fibre, high salt, high sugar, contains trans fat
- Nestle Golden Grahams – moderate fibre, high salt, high sugar, contains trans fat
- Kellogg's Frosties Chocolate, Kellogg's Hunny B's, Nestle Cinnamon Grahams, Nestle Honey Nut Cheerios – low fibre, high salt, high sugar
- Kellogg's Bar Simpson's Eat My Shorts, Kellogg's Choco Corn Flakes – low fibre, high salt, high sugar, contains trans fat.

Worst offenders, of cereals not specifically marketed to children included:

- Kellogg's Crispix, Kellogg's Crunchy Nut – low fibre, high salt, high sugar
- Kellogg's Cornflakes Banana Crunch, Kellogg's Crunchy Nut Clusters Milk Chocolate Curls, Jordans Country Crisp (four nut combo), Jordans Country Crisp (real strawberry, whole raspberry), Quaker Harvest Nut Crunch Collection – all contain a lot of saturated fat
- Kellogg's Crunchy Nut Red – moderate fibre, high salt, high sugar, contains trans fat
- Nestle Clusters – high fibre, high salt, high sugar, contains trans fat

- Kellogg's All Bran – Quaker Oat Krunchies – very high salt.

Consumers' Association (2004) *Cereal Offenders*. London.

Also available on the Consumers' Association web site:

www.which.net/campaigns/food/nutrition/0403cerealoffenders.pdf

School Milk

Cherie Morgan
School Milk Project Facilitator (To the children, Cherie is 'The Milk Lady'.)

How can we get milk into schools?

There are a number of options for schools. For example:

- Some schools choose to work with a local milk scheme, company or dairy who offer a complete package to schools including obtaining the funding from the European subsidy, milk delivery and collecting payments from parents.

- Some schools choose to claim the milk subsidy from the European Union by working with their Local Education Authority, and the school deals with the day-to-day administration of the milk.

- Some schools prefer to run their own scheme by liaising with their local suppliers. Any profit might be re-invested into the school. For example the milk might be sold within the tuck shop. Some tuck shops might offer a glass of milk and toast as package for a fixed price, making a profit on the toast but not on the milk.

- Some school caterers take responsibility for providing milk and deal with the related administration.

If a school is thinking about introducing school milk into their schools they should look at The School Milk Project website (www.schoolmilk.co.uk) or contact the Catering Services Department at their Local Education Authority.

What is the role of a School Milk Project facilitator?

Facilitators are there to work with everyone, the schools, the LEAs and the dairies. Our aim is to make milk available to every child, so that parents can choose whether they want their child to have milk. I am responsible for contacting all primary schools in this area. I ask the LEA to send letters to schools introducing myself. I phone the schools to make an appointment with the head teacher, administrator or healthy schools coordinator. We talk through whether the school has a milk scheme, and if they don't we discuss the reasons. We decide which option might be the most viable for that particular school environment by considering all the pros and cons. I might ask, "Is there space for a fridge? Are you aware of the anticipated number of empty milk cartons? Have we got bins available? Can we make sure that the bins are lined so that we don't get milk spillages? Where are you going to distribute the milk and how is it going to fit in with the day-to-day running of the school? Have we got other members of staff 'on side'? If staff are against it, it's going to be difficult to run an effective scheme without complications. If that means coming back and talking to a group of staff on another day, then I'm happy to do that and ask about their questions and concerns, and see if I can answer them. Staff can be worried that the milk distribution might take up the whole of the break time, and we might discuss allowing milk monitors to leave class early, followed by the children who are having milk, and then the rest. In this way all the children have a playtime. Some schools use the 'milk time' as a useful preliminary to the next lesson because it is calms the children. My work also includes visiting schools who have a milk scheme in place, but who are experiencing difficulties.

Could you give me some examples of how milk has been successfully introduced into schools?

A large primary school took part in the annual School Milk Week, organized by the Dairy Industry Alliance and the Milk Development Council, which encourages schools to be nominated to receive free milk for a day. As a follow-up to this, I went to meet the school administrator who was keen to introduce a regular milk scheme. I talked through the different options and the school decided to work with the local company Cool Milk at School. I put them in touch with Cool Milk at School who sent letters to the school to be forwarded to the parents. Interested parents responded to Cool

Milk at School agreeing to be invoiced for their children's milk. The company supplied the school with a free fridge, ordered the milk and organized the delivery of 1/3 pint cartons with straws. The school appointed milk monitors, who were originally supervised by the school administrator. The school administrator helped to promote the milk by writing articles for the school newsletter, organizing a display in the school entrance lobby and encouraging new parents to join the scheme at new parents' evenings. Today about 25% of the pupils are having milk and that, in this area, is pretty good.

The family liaison officer for another school approached me because she was concerned about the nutritional intake of the pupils. It was decided that the school would buy the milk themselves from the local dairy and sell it as part of a healthy tuck shop that included fruit and healthy biscuits. The family liaison officer promoted the plan to the children in advance, and initially served the milk for a couple of days a week. The children clearly enjoyed the milk, and looked forward to it, and so the school now offer milk every day. On some days the family liaison officer gets the children to make milk shakes with fresh fruit, giving them the opportunity to try something different. Through the school council, she has got the children involved in selling the milk. The children pay for the milk on a daily basis and the dairy weekly invoices the school. In this instance I was able to persuade the dairy to supply a fridge to the school. This isn't always possible, but sometimes a dairy will supply a fridge in return for gradual re-payment by increasing the cost of a carton of milk by a penny over a set period of time.

Useful Information

The School Milk Scheme and School Milk Project

The School Milk Scheme allows funding for school milk to be obtained from European Union subsidies by Local Education Authorities. The School Milk Project is an organization that enables primary schools to manage the practicalities of ordering and distributing the milk. The School Milk Project is a non-profit making organization funded by the Milk Development Council, employing facilitators throughout most of England.

Dairy Council

The Dairy Council produces a range of resources about milk and dental care, including information about the School Milk Scheme.

The Dairy Council
164 Shaftesbury Avenue
London
WC2H 8HL
Tel. 020 739 54030

www.milk.co.uk

Milk Development Council

The Milk Development Council runs the School Milk Project and can advise schools about which local dairies are willing to deliver school milk.

Milk Development Council
Stroud Road
Cirencester
GL7 6JN
Tel. 01285 646500

www.mdc.co.uk

National Osteoporosis Society

One in every three women, and one in every twelve men in the UK will have osteoporosis, which means porous bones, over the age of 50. Every three minutes someone in the UK breaks a bone because of osteoporosis. One particularly important preventative strategy is to develop strong bones during the growing years through a good intake of calcium. The best sources of calcium are milk and dairy products such as cheese and yoghurt. The National Osteoporosis Society has a wealth of information and educational materials.

National Osteoporosis Society
Camerton
Bath
BA2 OPJ

Tel. 01761 471771

www.nos.org.uk

School milk announcement

In 2005 the Department of Health announced that school milk must be free to children whose families receive certain welfare benefits.

Water in School

Gill Aitken
Healthy Schools Coordinator

It was by being part of the Healthy Schools network that I learnt about the importance of making water available to children. We had two water fountains and a couple of taps, but we'd had some very hot summers and it wasn't very convenient having children 'up and down' to get water all the time. I discussed the issue with staff and our school council, and everyone agreed that it would be a good idea to increase the availability of water in our school.

Firstly we bought some plastic bottles, the type used for 'sport drinks', from a local drink factory that gave us a good deal on price. These were labelled with the children's names, and if they were lost or broken the child replaced them with a similar bottle from home. However, much later, at a healthy schools network meeting someone suggested that there could be health and safety problems with repeated use of a bottle that's really only meant for single use. For example, they might not be washed out properly and if the components became loose they could choke. Certainly some of our children were still using the bottle given to them a year before. So we decided to re-think our water strategy.

We considered having a dispenser of filtered water. We found a company that gave us two to trial, one for the staff and one for the children. The children's was emptied on the first day so we decided that it would be too expensive, and we also didn't want the children to become rarefied about what water they would drink. If they got used to filtered water, they wouldn't want tap water, and then we'd have another problem.

We received a flyer from a plastics company advertising purpose built water bottles for schools. They look like the kind of bottles that can be fixed to a bicycle. They are more robust, with a wider lid, than the bottles we were using. Our Parents Teachers Association (PTA), the Friends of Selsted School, paid for three boxes of 48 bottles, with red, light blue or dark blue lids – the three house colours. A member of staff wrote the names on each bottle with indelible ink and the children carried them in their matching house-coloured bags.

The PTA also agreed to fund two new water fountains to replace the old ones. The children have written about the water bottles and the lovely new fountains in the school newsletter. They are thrilled to have these things. The fountains are so easy to use, and the children are very aware that plentiful sips of water are helping them. The staff are also drinking more water, because we purchased a water dispenser for the staff room, and the children can see that the staff are drinking water.

Of course there were some concerns along the way. Some staff worried that increasing water might mean more children going to the toilet more of the time, but this hasn't been a problem. Here we are flexible about letting children go to the toilet when they need. Things to look out for are children who don't want to go to the toilet at school, or children who are frightened to drink in case they need the toilet in lesson time. When the bottles arrived it was a novelty of course. Some sucked on them like babies' bottles as comforters, but this ceased pretty quickly as pupils were reminded to use them sensibly.

When the children are doing PE on the field, they all bring their water bottles out with them and sit them on the bench, and if they want a drink they have one. When walking back to class they might stop at a fountain. They use both. We have stacking, lightweight plastic baskets in the classrooms where the children put their bottles in the morning. This means that they are in a central place, but accessible. Parents have been very good. They wash the bottles out and ensure that the children bring them each morning. If a bottle is lost we charge £1.50 for a replacement.

Although it's difficult to prove, the children definitely perform a little better when they are able to drink plenty of water. Sometimes children don't realize that they need a drink. Everyone thinks that it's worthwhile, and I can't see a situation where we'd go back to having less accessible water."

Useful Information

Water is Cool in School Campaign

The Water is Cool in School Campaign was set up in 2000 to promote awareness about the health benefits of drinking water, and to promote access to fresh drinking water in schools.

Water is Cool in School Campaign
c/o Enuresis Resource and Information Centre
34 Old School House
Britannia Road
Kingswood
Bristol
BS15 8DB

Tel. 0117 960 3060

www.wateriscoolinschool.org.uk

Water for Health

Water for Health is an information resource supported by Water UK for anyone interested in water and health.

Water UK
1 Queen Anne's Gate
London
SW1H 9BT

Tel. 020 7344 1866

www.water.org.uk/waterforhealth

Drinking Water Inspectorate

The Drinking Water Inspectorate regulates public water supplies in England and Wales. They can advise about the quality of local water. Their web site includes a link to a children's web site Water4Life.

Drinking Water Inspectorate
55 Whitehall
London
SW1A 2EY

www.dwi.gov.uk

Cookery Club

Carmen Flynn
Healthy Schools Coordinator

The cookery club was originally suggested by our Year 5 teacher who thought that it would be an attractive, fun activity for the children. The idea coincided with a concern that many of our children don't have a healthy diet and a number take Ritalin. The cookery club is an after school club which runs from 3.15 to 4.15 pm once a week. Year 5 children can join the cookery club for half a term. This means that about a dozen children sign up for about six or seven sessions and by the end of the year all the Year 5 children have had the opportunity to join. The ingredients are provided by the school and the children take the food home.

We started with some very simple ideas such as decorating cakes using ready bought cakes, icing, cherries and hundreds and thousands. We had fruit tasting sessions and brought in pomegranates, star fruit, kiwi fruit and so on. The children had to describe the fruit in any way they liked, except they weren't allowed to say, "Yuk!" This encouraged them to find new words, and afterwards they made fruit kebabs. Similarly we had tasting of a food and its vegetarian alternative. The children had to work out which was the vegetarian option. Another time we made eggs into mice. Staff brought in hard-boiled eggs, the children cut them in half, added ham triangles for ears and raisins for eyes and presented them on a bed of lettuce.

It was agreed that we could use the school kitchens, and the cookery club became a little more adventurous making scones, pizza, sausage rolls, flans, sandwiches and fruit salads. When making fruit salads, the children often have the idea that they have to have every fruit in their fruit salad, that they have to stick to a rigid plan, and so we talk about them choosing the fruit which their family likes. We make the fruit salad using orange juice. The most successful thing we make is pizza. At the moment we provide pizza bases, though the cook has recently agreed that we could make up a batch of dough and make pizza from scratch in future. The children prepare all the toppings, and then decided which they are going to put on their own pizza.

Of course you learn as you go along. The first time we made fruit flans, using a sponge base with fruit on top, the children's jelly had almost set in the jug before they were able to pour it on so we had chopped up jelly on some of them! Also the first time we made scones we had flour everywhere and the children put too much milk in the dough! It took us a long time to clear up! So the lesson we have learnt is that we, the staff, add the water for the children.

In the cookery club, the first thing that is emphasised is hygiene, not always one of the children's priorities! A number of children have never used a knife and fork properly, and they have never seen many of the utensils being used. We show them how to hold a knife the right way up and they learn how to share the equipment with others. We talk about what type of fruit we have got, where it has come from. What are we eating, carbohydrate or protein? Should we mix them up? A child might say that they know someone on the Atkins diet, and I might ask, "Do you think dieting is right?" We have introduced a booklet about recipes, spending money on food and calculating the change which links to maths. A lot of what we do links to PSHE, and they develop skills of washing up, sweeping and stacking. Quite often the children will nominate a member of staff to receive a gift of food. Or if someone's missing, and they have extra pizza, they might decide to take it to the head teacher. All this work culminates in Year 5 producing a spread for the Year 6 graduation ceremony. Pupils plan the menu, buy the food and prepare it in designated areas before presenting it beautifully, with drinks, to the school guests.

We get good feedback from the parents. For one little lad, it was an incentive to come to school. In Year 5 the children move from lower playground to upper playground, as part of the upper school. He had this fear that the children were going to be 'big and horrible' although some of the older children had been in the lower playground with him the year before. His mum told us that he liked to cook, and so we ensured that he got into the next cookery club and he was much happier. All the children enjoy it, and some try to come back to join the group a second time. In future we are hoping to be able to incorporate the produce from the school's fruit and vegetable garden.

Useful Information

Focus on Food

Focus on Food is a campaign led by the Royal Society for the Encouragement of Arts and Waitrose to improve practical food education in schools. The initiative includes a cooking bus, a mobile food preparation classroom, which visits schools. Staffed by qualified and experienced food education teachers, it enables pupils to prepare a range of dishes. Focus on Food also supplies a range of resources such as recipes, teaching materials and research.

Focus on Food
Waitrose
South Industrial Area
Bracknel
Berkshire
RG12 8YA
Tel. 01344 824114

www.waitrose.com/about/children_education/focusonfood.asp

Cook Club

www.nutrition.org.uk/cookclub

The British Nutrition Foundation's Cook Club includes suitable recipes for primary school cooking.

Reasons to cook with children

20 reasons to cook with children:

- development of gross motor skills
- development of manipulative skills
- development of hand to eye coordination
- science learning e.g. dissolving, freezing, melting
- maths learning e.g. weights, measures
- decision making
- learning about different cultures
- observation skills
- learning to listen to sounds
- identifying tastes
- using smell
- exploring textures
- extending language
- sharing skills and teamwork
- coping with problems
- developing patience
- organizational skills
- learning about origins of food
- menu planning
- creativity.

Dare, A. and O'Donovan, M. (1996) *A Practical Guide to Child Nutrition.* Cheltenham: Stanley Thornes (Publishers) Ltd.

Fruit in School

Carol Manton
Family Liaison Officer

What was your initial aim?

We set up the fruit bar to encourage the children to eat more fruit. There has always been a policy at our school that children could eat only fruit at playtime, but because of the location of the school it is difficult to get fresh fruit unless you go into town or to one of the big supermarkets. East Kent Healthy Schools supported us, and now we have a fruit delivery nearly every day.

How does the fruit bar run?

The washed fruit is delivered in trays. Our cook lets us keep it in the fridge. In the morning, I put the fruit out onto a trolley. We drew up a rota for Year 6 children because we wanted them to have some responsibility. After assembly two Year 6 children take the trolley to the playground. The children form two lines. The Year 6 children sell the fruit and they phone the greengrocer to order what they think they will need for the next day. Children can still bring fruit from home if they want to, but we've been going for a year now and it's still as popular as when we first started.

How did you decide on the price of the fruit?

We weren't bothered about making a profit. Initially the greengrocer sold us a piece of fruit for 8 pence, and we sold it at 10 pence. This was mostly because the children only have 15 minutes for playtime and having a 10 pence piece is easy for children and their parents. The greengrocer has recently put the price up to 10 pence so next term we are going to have to increase the price to 12 pence to cover the cost of the few pieces of fruit which we have to throw away.

How popular is fruit in school?

Most of the children have fruit, across both infants and juniors. After the summer holidays we wondered how many children would remember their 10 pence on the first day, and nearly all did. We were astounded! We've had mums say to us that they will give their child 10 pence for fruit, "... but they won't eat it." And they do! I think that seeing other children eating the fruit encourages others. We've never had any complaints that we are not selling crisps or other tuck shop items.

Which fruit works best in school?

We tend to stick with red and green apples, pears, bananas, satsumas and mandarin oranges. In the summer we have peaches and nectarines. Quite a few of our children have never tasted these fruits and want to know what they are. They ask for nectarines in winter and we explain about how some fruit is only available in certain seasons. In our school they love green apples, in another school they can't get enough bananas. Oranges are not a good idea. Children love them, but they take so long to peel and the children don't have enough time for this. Sticky fingers aren't a problem. Children wash their hands if they need to.

How do you deal with the waste?

We wanted a garden for our school, for the children to grow fruit and vegetables. So we got two composting bins from the recycling department of the local council. When we started the fruit bar we explained to the children that when they had finished their fruit they should put their cores and peelings into the composters, and they just do it. We have no litter problem. The compost will be going onto the garden.

How can schools introduce fruit into their schools?

Teachers might bring fruit into schools as part of science lessons, or ask a farmer to come and give a talk. I started by ringing around to find a local greengrocer who would deliver fruit at a reasonable cost. Schools need to find a greengrocer who is happy to deliver small quantities of good quality, washed fruit. We tell parents about the fruit bar through the school newsletter and talk about it with the children in assembly.

I wanted make the fruit bar as hassle free as possible because the staff have lots of other things to do besides asking children whether they want an apple or banana each day. So now we just put out a selection of fruit and the children buy what they want each day. I don't cut up the fruit, again, to keep things easy. Most children eat most of the fruit, there isn't much waste.

Useful Information

5-A-Day Programme

The 5-A-Day Programme is an initiative led by the Department of Health to encourage people to eat more fruit and vegetables. The 5-A-Day logo appears on a wide variety of brands, telling people that these foods can contribute to their five portions per day. The Department of Health produce a range of educational materials, such as posters and postcards, featuring 5-A-Day. See their web site www.5aday.nhs.uk.

School Fruit and Vegetable Scheme

The School Fruit and Vegetable Scheme is part of the 5-A-Day Programme. Details can be obtained through the 5-A-Day web site (www.5aday.nhs.uk).

Department of Health (2003) *The School Fruit and Vegetable Scheme*. London.

National School Fruit Scheme

The National School Fruit Scheme, part of the School Fruit and Vegetable Scheme, entitles four to six year old children in Local Education Authority maintained infant, primary and special schools to a piece of fruit or vegetable every day; the broader aims of the Scheme are to promote fruit eating across the whole-school. Much emphasis is placed on the need to integrate fruit and vegetables into children's culture by making it fun.

Department of Health (2004) *The National School Fruit Scheme*. London.

Available from Department of Health
PO Box 777
London
SE1 6XH
Tel. 0800 555 777

Free Fruit Initiative (Scotland)

The Free Fruit Initiative in Scotland provides one portion of fruit, three times a week, in primary schools.

www.scotland.gov.uk/Topics/Education/School-Education/18922/15774

Fruit Tuck Shops

Fruit Tuck Shops is a practical guide to planning and running a school tuck shop. It is based on research carried out by the University of Bristol and the Health Promotion Division of the National Assembly for Wales. Visit www.food.gov.uk/multimedia/pdfs/fruittuckwales.pdf or type the guide title into a search engine.

Grab 5!

Grab 5! is a project, led by Sustain, to encourage primary school pupils to eat more fruit and vegetables. Sustain carry out training, research, advise on policy and provide resources for schools.

www.sustainweb.org/grab5_index.asp

Food Dudes

Food Dudes is a research-based initiative developed by the University of Bangor to promote the consumption of fruit and vegetables among children. Their web site includes details of their research and, within the Related Information section, a comprehensive Staff Handbook showing how to run a Food Dude Healthy Eating Programme in school. The programme includes the use of videos, rewards, letters to children from the Food Dudes, home pack and educational support materials. The programme has three phases. Phase 1 lasts for 16 days and children are rewarded for every time they eat the required amount of fruit or vegetables. This works out at a maximum of 15 minutes per day. Phase 2 lasts for six months, whereby the rewards are reduced with the support of other educational resources, and Phase 3 is about schools sustaining the consumption of fruit and vegetables into the future.

www.fooddudes.co.uk

Growing Produce

Chris Ford
Teacher

We are an Eco-School which means that we meet a set of environmental criteria set by Environmental Campaigns (ENCAMS). We have developed an environmental code for the school, and have an annual action plan. This means that we look after our environment by recycling, saving water, turning off lights, putting litter in the bin and so forth. We recently won a gold award. Green Club was set up prior to us becoming an Eco-School, and continues to be a very important part of this work. It is a once a week after school club, for an hour, with eight to ten Year 4 children. We do jobs such as clearing leaves, planting flowers and looking after the flower-beds, and growing vegetables. We do whatever environmental jobs need doing at that time of the year.

A couple of years ago one of our local residents, who belongs to the local gardening club, offered to dig some vegetable plots for the Green Club. So we now have two plots of about 4 feet by 10 feet, and three raised beds, of about 6 feet square, in which we grow vegetables, as well keeping our flower gardens looking nice. We have a shed containing small sized rakes, spades, forks and wheelbarrows, and a couple of compost heaps. We have just bought three compost bins, which will be a bit easier. The Green Club ploughs everything back into the garden, including the fruit from playtime.

This year we've grown potatoes, cabbages, sweet corn, beetroot, courgettes, herbs, lettuces and French beans. We tried carrots but the ground doesn't seem to be good for those. Some produce, like lettuces, beetroot and herbs, are used in the school canteen. Sometimes the children take some home, sometimes we sell them to the staff and the money goes back into the Green Club funds. The school pays for some things, but we also fund ourselves through selling our produce. This year we sold our potatoes at the summer fair, and that money was put back into funding the Green Club.

What do you think are the benefits of the Green Club?

The whole idea of working together. A lot of children don't know where vegetables come from, and so they learn a lot about what they look like when they are growing and what to do with them. Most children are very interested in this, and we try to do everything organically which fits into our role as an eco-school. So it is both educational and social.

For the staff, what kind of planning goes into Green Club?

You need to be thinking in advance about what jobs the children can do. At the beginning of the year, when we start with a new class, we begin by wandering around the grounds. The children, with a bit of help, identify the jobs that they think need doing. Then it's a question of planning the jobs into the right time of the year, and thinking about what the children can and can't do. Every now and then we have an action day where parents come along and do the jobs that the children can't do such as clearing brambles or some of the work around the pond. The whole school can become involved sometimes. We had a day when parents came along with their children and we painted pots to put outside and planted tubs. Some of the things which you would like to grow, you can't because they are ready at the wrong time, such as in the summer holidays, so this needs to considered when planning.

What advice would you give to a school wanting to start a Green Club?

- Firstly you need a basic range of tools. I would advise a wheelbarrow, small/border trowels, forks and spades, watering cans and gloves for the children. Children's gloves are the hardest things to get at a reasonable price. Children's gloves are as expensive as very good quality adult ones, it is very difficult to get cheap ones. So we use adult ones which are really too big for them, but gloves are really important.

- Children need to bring old clothes, and wellies or sturdy boots.

- You need children that are interested. So I'd suggest an assembly or an event which introduces the idea to them, but you want to try to make it as if it was the children's own idea. If it's your idea, you can lose them. If they think it's their idea they get enthusiastic.

- Try to give the children a sense of ownership.

- We set ground rules at the beginning about how to care for the equipment, how to carry it, how to lay it down, how to put it away. We talk about safe behaviour, which includes that they must wear gloves.

What works particularly well?

The children loved growing potatoes. Last year each child had a tub of their own in which to grow potatoes, and later took them home. The children had to water them and look after them. We weighed the tubs to see who had the most in their tubs. Perhaps it worked well because each had their own tub rather than sharing, and the children like to be able to say, "We did that." When the children dug down, they were amazed to see all the potatoes below. Also, potatoes are quite 'showy' with plenty of top growth, I think they like 'showy' things, they liked the courgettes as well.

What are the challenges?

The main challenge is to really think about the jobs that the children can do. It's easy to think, "I can do that with the children helping," but then you find that they can't help. It's too hard, perhaps it's too heavy for them. It's really important to have smaller tools, because they really can't cope with standard tools. One of the hardest things is thinking about what to do if it's very wet and you can't go out. We usually look for environmentally useful jobs around the school e.g. posters about environmental issues.

Mud?

Mud – they love it! They have to take shoes off at the door, and dirty shoes go in a carrier bag.

Useful Information

Eco Schools

www.encams.org/aboutus/index.asp

England

Eco Schools
ENCAMS
Elizabeth
The Pier
Wigan
WN3 4EX

Scotland

Eco-Schools
Keep Scotland Beautiful
House Islay House
Livilands Lane
Stirling
FK8 2BG

Wales

Eco-Schools
Keep Wales Tidy Campaign
33/35 Cathedral Road
Cardiff
CF11 9HB

Northern Ireland

Eco-Schools
Tidy Northern Ireland
1st Floor, Studio A
89 Holywood Road
Belfast BT4 3BA

Eco Schools Newsletters

www.eco-schools.org/new/newsletters.htm

Soil Association

The Soil Association describes itself as 'the UK's leading campaigning and certification organisation for organic food and farming'. They have an education section on their web site including details about their Food for Life programme.

Soil Association
Bristol House
40-56 Victoria Street
Bristol
BS1 6BY

Tel. 0117 314 5000

www.soilassociation.org

Growing Schools

The Department for Education and Skills launched the Growing Schools website to support teachers who want to use the 'outdoor' classroom as a resource, for example, it includes a Seasonal Growing Calendar and advice on health and safety.

www.teachernet.gov.uk/growingschools

Community Gardens

Paul Boyce
Community Garden Manager

I run a community garden for the charity MIND (National Association for Mental Health) in Northdown Park. Adults and students with learning disabilities grow flowers and organic vegetables. Pupils from local primary schools occasionally visit. I take them on a walk around the garden, talk about the different plants, identify the vegetables and then they dig or pick them. Yesterday a class came and they dug up carrots, worked on the runner beans and then picked some to take back to school. The children love walking around, picking things off and tasting them.

From the point of the view of the students, it is hard to place students with learning disabilities into conventional work experience. Here, they can work with adults and get the idea of turning up and going to work, and contributing something useful. It is great when the children come because the adults, who might have problems such as long-term depression or schizophrenia, see the children enjoying themselves, and it helps to take them out of themselves. It is all supervised. It is nice for those with learning disabilities to be able to help the children who are less able than themselves. It gives them the feeling that they have something to offer.

A useful organisation for schools to know about is Thrive. They have community gardens in many areas that schools could visit. Thrive work with everyone from children to the elderly, using gardening as a form of therapy, rehabilitation, relaxation or education.

Useful Information

Thrive

Thrive describes itself as the national charity which enables disadvantaged, disabled and older people to participate fully in the social and economic life of the community. It has more than 1600 groups in the UK helping 60,000 people many of whom have sensory or physical impairments, learning difficulties or mental health needs.

Thrive – The Society for Horticultural Therapy Charity
The Geoffrey Udall Centre
Beech Hill
Reading
RG7 2AT

Tel. 0118 988 5688

www.thrive.org.uk

The County Council

Mark Sleep
Client Services Manager

If you wanted to encourage healthy eating in a school, what would you do?

I'd look at the menu and see if they have plenty of healthy items to choose from. We recently asked all schools in Kent if they would like to join the Kent County Council school meals contract, and about two-thirds, mostly primary schools, did. We consulted with schools and began a tendering process. We didn't specify portion size or nutritional content, but we said that the meals (a) had to comply with the national requirements (b) had to be compliant with the Kent Heartbeat Award (c) had to have due consideration of the Caroline Walker Trust Guidelines. We asked that the tenders should include both packed lunch and traditional two-course menus. Eventually the contract was awarded to Initial because they gave the best value for money. They provide a traditional two-course meal with additional items of carbohydrate, salad and a drink. The main challenge was keeping the iron content up and the fat content down, but we got there. Initial also have a nutritionist who visits schools, and they have some successful marketing initiatives that together have worked well. We monitor the school meals through six monitoring officers, who work with me to audit the contract on a continuous basis, and through Initial's own evaluations.

Which system of payment would you recommend for a primary school?

In Primary Schools where they are more likely to be having a limited, traditional style meal compared to Secondary Schools, and unless they have a successful pre-payment system, I'd go for a card, badge or cap with a bar code. The school collects the money, charges up the card and holds the information on a computer. The card covers a two-course meal and has the advantage of children not having to carry money. The system allows the school to see clearly who has paid and who has a free meal, whilst maintaining anonymity for children who have free school meals. The drawbacks are that small children can lose cards, which is why I think a badge or cap works better. Another factor is the local culture. If parents use cards, such as credit cards regularly, the children tend to adapt to a card system more easily. In some schools cash systems work better than card systems, because cash is the usual method of payment in their local community.

What about smart cards?

The idea of a smart card is that the pupils can put money into a system. They either use a swipe card, like a bank card, or a card with a microchip. With a swipe card all the information is held on the computer network within the school, with a smart card the information is held in the chip and the school has readers that will take information from the chip. The readers are held at the till or in a vending machine. The schools need to have re-charging machines into which pupils place money to charge their cards. Children who have free school meals can have a card that is credited for them on a daily basis.

The positive points about smart cards are:

- The school is able to control what the card is able to purchase. For example, the card can be programmed so that a child can only use it for a main meal, or it can contain a limit on the items that can be purchased from a vending machine, or it can only be used between certain times of the day. The card can be programmed to help a child stick to a special diet, or avoid foods to which they are allergic.

- Schools can add bonus points if they wish to reward pupils. For example, children can receive bonus points for choosing healthy options and these can be linked to a reward such as vouchers.

- They speed up service.

- They give the school information about what pupils are eating and can be a useful aid to school food management.

- Children like them because they are 'cool'. Some children like not having to carry money, and this can reduce bullying.

- Parents can have confidence about what the money is being spent on. The system allows parents to send a cheque, rather than cash, if they prefer. Parents can receive feedback on what the child is eating.

- The cards can contain other information and be used as library cards, access to photocopying, registration and so forth.

The negative points about smart cards are:

- The cards with photographs are expensive, as are the special tills and re-charging machines. Some schools buy blank cards and add the photographs. If cards are lost, they are quite expensive for the child or parent to replace.

- If the child loses a card, and is entitled to a free school meal, they need to be issued with a temporary card and this is very time consuming.

- If the reader at the till crashes, there is no alternative way of making transactions.

Smart cards probably work better in larger schools, and in schools where there is not a cash system operating simultaneously.

What are the challenges facing school catering?

We do take an awful lot of flack, which I feel is misdirected, but it sells newspapers. In the recent story arguing how little was spent on school meals, the journalists compared the price of a day's food for prisoners with a single meal in a school. So they weren't comparing the same thing. You also have to remember that children are only at school for one meal a day for 191 days of the year. So it's the parents who need to support what the school does and vice versa. If the parents are doing well, the school needs to support them.

Why don't school meals use more fresh vegetables?

We use frozen vegetables for convenience. We would like to use more local produce, but who is going to go to the farmer to get his cabbages, and what happens when his cabbages run out? Does he provide sweet corn, because many children don't like cabbage? If you give them beans, they won't eat them, but they will eat peas. To get children to eat something, you have to give them something they will eat. Also, we have 187 schools to which meals need to be transported. If you have ever eaten cauliflower when it's been in a hot box for half an hour you wouldn't want to eat it again. So it's also about acceptability and what children will eat.

What about the argument that if vegetables are not presented to children, they don't try them?

Within our school meals contract, a salad must be available and some of the children do tend to go for it. They don't like tomatoes too much, but I think that's a taste thing generally with young children. Is it the caterer's job to educate the children, or is it the school's job to help the caterer provide food through educating the children in their eating habits, or is it the parents' job? The caterers are carrying out a commercial operation and, yes, they will send out nutritionists and, yes, it is in their interest to sell more meals, but if you're going to serve up liver and bacon once a week you might as well give up because the children won't eat it, and they still won't be getting their iron requirement. Until the Government is prepared to spend more money, the service can't leap forward. Schools which do particularly well are usually the ones with 'whole-school approaches' and School Nutrition Action Groups (SNAGS) or the equivalent.

Useful Information

The Caroline Walker Trust

The Caroline Walker Trust was founded in 1988 after the death of one of the UK's most distinguished nutritionists who campaigned for better nutrition. The Trust has produced guidelines for the nutrient content of school meals.

Caroline Walker Trust (1992) *Nutritional Guidelines for School Meals. Report of an Expert Working Group.* London.

The Caroline Walker Trust
PO Box 61
St Austell, PL26 6YL

Tel: 01726 844107

www.cwt.org.uk

Feed Me Better Campaign

Jamie Oliver's Feed Me Better Campaign aims to make radical changes to the school meals system. Further information can be found at www.feedmebetter.com.

Nutritional Standards for School Meals

See the Department for Education and Skills website (www.dfes.gov.uk) for revised nutritional standards due to be published in 2006.

Healthy Lunch Boxes

Jill Flavin
Healthy Schools Coordinator

We weren't happy about what the parents were putting into the children's lunch boxes, and so we started by banning fizzy drinks, partly because of the mess. Some children had never looked at a piece of fruit, and so we introduced a healthy fruit tuck shop at break time, and we also began a healthy breakfast scheme. Then we tackled the lunch boxes more directly. Around the time that the reception children join the school, before they start having lunches at school, the parents are invited to a meeting at the school. We ask someone from Healthy Schools to talk about what to put into lunch boxes, what not to put in and healthy options. Parents are given leaflets to take away. At the start of the curriculum we talk about healthy foods and healthy sandwiches. Throughout the year most of the children will make different sorts of sandwiches during the lesson times.

During Sport and Health Week we have a healthy food day where the whole day is given over to making healthy sandwiches in the school hall. Someone from Healthy Schools gives a talk to each class and afterwards, one class at a time, they come into the hall to make their healthy sandwiches. The idea recognizes that children have some input with their parents, in saying what they like and don't like in their sandwiches. Some parents come to help with the day. It has to be a military style operation, as we need to build in breaks, prepare for the next class and ensure that the ingredients are fresh all the time. Guess who has to do the shopping! It is exhausting, but very valuable. All the children go home with a sandwich in greaseproof paper or a little plastic bag. It is a wonderful day and everybody loves it.

We haven't had any problems with parents. About two thirds of our children have packed lunches. With some parents if you don't keep reminding them, they fall back into old ways. For example, we had a child who brought three packets of crisps for their lunch, others who have no drink, some who bring too little food. Of course you have to be very diplomatic. I might say to a parent, "Would it be possible to put a piece of fruit in Jane's lunch box tomorrow as she was still a little hungry after she had finished her lunch today?" I know that sometimes it is awkward. Sometimes, as a parent, you go to prepare the lunch box and you find you haven't got anything, so you just scrape together what you can. That's fair enough, but we get concerned if we think that the lunch is consistently inappropriate.

Our general guidelines for healthy lunch boxes are that they supply enough food, a variety of food, a drink and preferably a piece of fruit. We would like to see foods from each food group, without overloading the carbohydrate and sweet things. If a teacher wanted to try to improve the lunch boxes in their school I would recommend that they talk to the children first, then organize a meeting with parents and involve the Healthy Schools team as they have the expertise.

Useful Information

British Sandwich Association

The British Sandwich Association has a recipe web page containing interesting ideas for sandwiches on their web site: www.sandwich.org.uk/Recipies.asp

Food Standards Agency

The Food Standards Agency is an independent food safety watchdog set up by an Act of Parliament in 2000 to protect the public's health and consumer interests in relation to food. They have carried out a survey into school lunch boxes and provide useful tips on their web site.

Jefferson, A. and Cowbrough, K. (2003) *School Lunch Box Survey 2004*, London, FSA/Community Nutrition Group

www.food.gov.uk/multimedia/pdfs/lunchsurvey.pdf

The Food Standards Agency provides top tips for a healthier lunch box at www.food.gov.uk/news/newsarchive/2004/sep/toplunchboxtips

Food Standards Agency
Aviation House
125 Kingsway
London
WC2B 6NH

Tel. 020 7276 8000

www.food.gov.uk

Ideas for healthy lunch boxes

The Kent Health and Education Partnership recommend the following ideas for lunch boxes:

- Try to vary the bread used in sandwiches.

- Sandwiches can be shaped using cutters, triple-deckers, catherine wheels, diamonds or fingers.

- Avoid sandwiches every day. Try soup in a small vacuum flask or pasta or potato salad or mini quiches.

- Peel fresh fruit and cut into bite sized pieces.

- Make kebabs from fresh fruit using a cocktail stick or thin length of celery.

- Include a small surprise sometimes.

- Some good ideas to include are: mini box of raisins, dried fruits such as apricots or dates, pumpkin seeds, unsweetened popcorn, carrot/cucumber sticks with dip, seedless grapes, cherry tomatoes, mini bananas, apple wedges tossed in lemon juice, peeled Satsuma, fingers of cheese, strawberries.

- Cut an apple in half, scoop out the core, spread the hollow with peanut butter, put the apple together again, wrap in foil.

Healthy School Catering

Mog Marchant
Catering Manager

We provide meals for a junior and infant school, and our aim is to ensure that our students have the best quality food at prices that are as reasonable as possible. Our catering is independent so, as long as we work within the recommended guidelines, we can choose what to provide. Five years ago teachers were reporting that some pupils were 'hyper' after lunch because of eating excess sugar and caffeine, and lethargic towards the end of the day as their blood sugar dropped. So healthy catering became one of a number of healthy changes, supported by the whole school.

We promote healthy eating through 'the back door' rather than trying to force health down the pupils' throats. For example, we use low fat spread on sandwiches and jacket potatoes. We only spread on one side of the sandwich so that we are cutting the fat by 50% on every sandwich, and we make all our own sandwich fillings using low fat mayonnaise. About 70% of our vegetables are fresh and cooked without salt.

Our pricing structure is biased against snack items and we subsidise the main meals that are £1.47 for primary school pupils, and £1.57 for secondary pupils at the moment. Today's main meal was lamb and tomato pie. We know that the lamb is high quality and low fat. We don't add extra fat and we season it ourselves. Alternatively there was macaroni cheese, for which we used a mix of low fat and standard Cheddar. With this, the pupils had new potatoes, fresh cabbage, fresh parsnips, home made low sugar rice pudding made with semi-skimmed milk and fruit. Tomorrow there will be whole roast chicken leg, fresh carrots, fresh broccoli, roast potatoes, apple sponge and custard. We also offer jacket potatoes with one filling for 85p or with two fillings for £1 every day. A deli bar serves different sandwiches, wraps, baguettes and bagels, all with freshly made fillings. We also make pizza, pasta, coleslaw, salads and salad pots for serving every day, and have special theme days, summer specials and Christmas dinners.

80%, out of 1000 girls, use the school catering at some time of the day, and most of the rest bring packed lunches. A few don't eat and a few eat at break but not at lunch. A small minority eat chips and beans. We make sure that the beans are low sugar and the chips are large and thick and cooked in oil. Chips are a snack item and cost 90p. The most popular food tends to vary; wraps are going well at the moment, and the main meal is always popular.

We have a school catering committee, which includes myself, girls from each year group, and some Heads of Year. Sometimes the girls might ask why we don't have chocolate and fizzy drinks, and we explain that we are trying to encourage healthier eating. These days, five years in, we don't get many requests for chips, chocolate and coke etc. When we first took over there were vending machines for coke, chocolate and crisps. The last one went last year. The deal, agreed through the catering committee, was that we would offer the girls confectionery at breakfast, break and in the afternoons, but not at lunch. We offer low fat crisps, Kit-Kats and cereal bars. There are no rules about bringing snacks in from home, they wouldn't be enforceable, but in general most girls drink plain or fruit flavoured water and bringing snacks from home isn't really an issue.

If any school wanted to succeed with healthy catering we would suggest that they start by setting up a committee with their students to find out what the students don't like. They might be surprised. Sometimes staff think that most students are going to ask for chips and beans every day, but in reality they don't. Some catering staff can have preconceived ideas about what girls and boys will and won't eat. Some think that cooking is just heating up ready prepared food. You have to break down these barriers; if you can make the food look nice, smell nice, be of good quality, fill them up, at a price students can afford, you are half way there. Staff can become so demoralized if pupils don't like the food they are serving, and the students are only there because they have no choice. The catering needs to be looked at afresh. Schools need to do tasting evenings and get on board with their customers – the pupils. For example, wraps are really 'big' at the moment, so jump on the bandwagon and bring a deli bar in. If the school has carbonated drinks, reduce them to two choices and bring in substitutes like flavoured water and sugar free options. If there are ten lines of confectionary, reduce it to four, explain why, and substitute with cereal bars, low fat biscuits and other options. Change things slowly, and offer replacements. Don't just get rid of things, or you will just annoy everybody. It is also really important that the catering staff treat the students as customers and the atmosphere is like a restaurant. We have a very good relationship with our customers, they call us by our first names, they come in to chat. We have a team of 13 staff who love their jobs and are proud to be standing behind the food that they are serving.

We are lucky to have whole-school commitment; our success is built on it. Staff eat the same food as the pupils on a regular daily basis. The dining hall is a common area enjoyed by all. We aren't required to make a profit, just to break even. The teachers have noticed a difference in the afternoon lessons, and enjoy the food themselves. Most of the girls don't give the cooking a thought. They sometimes comment on the poor quality of food and higher prices elsewhere. Most don't even know that they are eating healthily. They just know that they like it."

Useful Information

Catering for Health

The British Nutrition Foundation and the Food Standards Agency have published a guide for teaching healthier catering practices.

British Nutrition Foundation (2001) *Catering for Health: a Guide for Teaching Healthier Catering Practices*, London, The Stationery Office ISBN 01124 30678.

Local Food Works

www.localfoodworks.org

Local Food Works has produced a comprehensive guide of local food directories, with links to The Organic Directory, farmers markets, farm shops, local food link organisations, producer marketing groups and whole food co-ops. By looking in their 'information library' schools can source local and organic produce from local farmers.

Soil Association

The Soil Association has produced *Food for Life: The Soil Association School Meals Action Pack* which provides practical guidance to those wishing to improve school meals.

Soil Association
Bristol House
40-56 Victoria Street
Bristol
BS1 6BY
Tel. 0117 314 5000

www.soilassociation.org

Kent Heartbeat Award Scheme

Georgina Ayin
Nutritionist

In order to get a Kent Heartbeat Award schools have to pass a hygiene assessment undertaken by their local environmental health officer. It is the officer who nominates the school to be assessed for the Kent Heartbeat Award. At this point I liaise with the school caterer and sometimes the head teacher, and observe kitchen activities. On the basis of this, I will work with a school to bring about changes in the menu, the snacks and any displayed information.

The school has to meet these criteria:

- 100% of the eating area must be smoke free (which all schools are)

- One third of the dishes on the menu must be healthy, that is low in saturated fat, salt and sugar.

- All food handlers must have received food hygiene training.

- All premises must comply with food safety law.

- The award must be promoted within the establishment.

The Award is of interest to Ofsted inspectors and can be used to monitor contract catering services where appropriate. Head teachers report anecdotally that nutritious options seem to be related to better concentration amongst the children and peace of mind for parents, and it is for these reasons that they consider it to be an asset to their school.

Owning a Heartbeat Award is only the start of the relationship because thereafter we work with the school to maintain and improve standards further. For example we can supply cooks, advice and promotional materials in order to support healthy eating weeks/days, give talks about nutrition and so forth.

If a school would like more information, they should contact their local Environmental Health Department and ask to speak to the Heartbeat Contact.

Useful Information

Heartbeat Award

The Heartbeat Award for Caterers was developed in 1987 by the Health Education Authority and the Chartered Institute of Environmental Health. The Award was given on the basis of an assessment of catering premises, the provision of healthy options on the menu, having at least one third of the dining area as non-smoking and at least one third of the catering staff trained in food hygiene. In 1992 when the Government launched a major drive to prevent the coronary heart disease, the Heartbeat Award was devolved to local level.

Kent Heartbeat Award

The Kent Heartbeat Award aims to encourage caterers, across the public and private sectors, to promote safe food, smoke-free dining areas and offer healthier options on the menu. It has a steering group representing local dietitians, dental care, health promotion, the health authority and local authority. Details can be found on the web site www.kenthealthyschools.org/healthyeating. html

British Heart Foundation

The British Heart Foundation funds research into heart disease and provides educational materials for schools, health professionals and the general public.

British Heart Foundation
14 Fitzhardinge Street
London
W1H 6DH

Tel. 020 7935 0185

www.bhf.org.uk

School Nutrition Action Group

 Gillian Trumble
Advanced Skills Teacher

Our group was set up as part of the Healthy Schools initiative. Although we don't call our group a School Nutrition Action Group (SNAG), it is a group that was set up to promote healthier eating in school. We decided to look at what we were eating during the day and wondered if we could improve it. What would happen if we stopped eating junk food and started to eat healthier options? I became involved because my role is citizenship and getting pupils to participate, and to make sensible choices, is a major part of this work. The group consists of pupils from across the different year groups, a parent and a governor. We meet on a regular basis and look at schemes to encourage healthier eating.

The vending machines were one of the first things to go. We introduced snacks from the dining room instead. These are homemade biscuits, buns, fruit and pizza slices which are healthier than things like sticky chewy bars. The boys just took it in their stride. It wasn't the big issue we thought it might be. Since then, the pupils have written questionnaires and found out what other pupils eat and what they would like to eat. This has given us some statistics. We have prepared a brochure, an A5 sheet, about food for the new Year 7 pupils. It emphasises that we have the responsibility to make choices, and it shows the benefits of choosing food wisely. A couple of students have recently written to food suppliers to see if we can make fruit available at break time, and we are also trying to promote bottled water in classrooms because, from a learning point of view, it is better for them.

An important area of our work is negotiating with the catering company and trying to get healthy options. At lunchtime we have introduced a salad bar, there is always a selection of fruit and we've limited chips to three times a week. We've achieved a reduction in the selling of sweets by limiting their sale to break time, and not lunchtime. We've been pushing to reduce the availability of highly coloured, fizzy drinks because they reduce concentration in the afternoons. The catering company have agreed to phase them out, and we are getting more water, milk and flavoured water.

What have been your greatest challenges?

Chips were the priority issue. Boys here wanted to get straight into the dining room at break and lunch time and stuff themselves with chips, almost as comfort food. Then we looked at fresh fruit and vegetables and the way that food is produced. We have a super catering lady who now checks that we have fresh vegetables, freshly served up, and more boiled and jacket potatoes. Of course another challenge is that we are up against the big advertisers and the need for caterers to make profits. We have to consider that our initiatives also have to encourage children to buy, and making profit from children's lunches presents us with an ethical issue.

Another challenge is the problem of time. In a school where issues relating to teaching, learning and raising standards take up a lot of time, the issues of healthy eating can get sidelined. However, I feel that the two are connected in that good eating habits can promote higher levels of achievement.

What have been your greatest successes?

The reduction in chip consumption, followed by the cold salad bar, which provides alternatives to the main hot meal. We have cellophane boxes containing rice and pasta salads and prepared fruit pieces, as well as sandwiches, baguettes and rolls. Also, it's great to see more staff eating a healthier lunch.

Why do you think the group has been so successful?

I think that the pupil participation is key. The ideas come from them rather than us dictating to them. They are taking the initiative. They have done the research, and they can see that something might be a good idea. Also, I have sent a letter home to let pupils and families know what is going on and asking for their support. I haven't had much feedback from parents so far, but I'd like to follow that up. We've also discussed this work in assemblies. The diet has improved because of the changes, but we're not there yet. You have to keep on top of this. If you're not on top of it, it could easily slip back again. It's an on-going project.

Useful Information

School Nutrition Action Groups (SNAGS)

The Health Education Trust, who have pioneered SNAGS, describe them as school based alliances in which staff, pupils and caterers, supported by health and education professionals work together to review and expand the range of food and drink in order to increase uptake of a healthier diet and ensure consistent messages from the curriculum and the food service. For more information, see the SNAG web site at www.healthedtrust.com/pages/snag.htm.

Health Education Trust
18 High Street
Broom
Alcester
Warwickshire
B50 4HJ

www.healthedtrust.com

Analysis of common snack foods

Trading Standards were invited by the Kent Healthy Schools Programme Healthy Eating Strategy Group to analyse common snack foods.

A packet or bar of:

- Walkers potato crisps contains 181 calories
- Hula hoops contains 176 calories
- Wotsits contains 114 calories
- Quavers contains 101 calories
- Kit Kat contains 128 calories
- Wagon Wheel contains 163 calories
- Harvest contains 87 calories
- Fruit winders contain 70 calories
- Twix contains 287 calories.

The School Council and the Healthy Schools Working Group

Sharon Bremner
Healthy Schools Coordinator

The School Council consists of two representatives from each junior class and from our Year 2 infants, myself and our special needs coordinator. The representatives are elected by their class each term, and the Council meets monthly. Any child can write a suggestion about any aspect of the school, and place it in a box in their classroom. Their class representative brings the suggestions to the School Council. Although I help to facilitate the Council, it is their meeting. We want the children in our school to realize that they can make a difference that they have a voice, that they are important and to learn the way to make changes.

In January 2002 I became the healthy schools coordinator with the support of the Healthy Schools team at the East Kent Health Promotion Service. I invited our school governors, school nurse, milkman, Mrs Huntly who runs the breakfast club and our special needs coordinator to join our Healthy Schools Working Group. In the last 12 months we have replaced the crisps, snacks and biscuits with a fruit and milk bar, introduced water into classrooms, instigated the brain gym which consists of exercises to promote concentration and learning, introduced a gardening club, a vegetable plot, obtained a greenhouse, improved the school environment by planting flowers and raised the standards of cleanliness and attendance. The School Council and the Healthy Schools Working Group have both helped these changes to come about.

Last September a decision was taken by the head teacher that we were going to stop all crisps, chocolates and biscuits at break time, and introduce fruit instead. This was partly about health, but it was also because of the litter around the playground. The deputy head attended the School Council and told the children about the decision, and explained why we were going to do this. So it was the children who took this back to their classes to let everybody know rather than the head teacher just saying, "This is what's happening." We didn't have any war, which we were expecting! No problem from parents either. It went very smoothly.

Later, when the children were given their free water bottles, some of the children lost their bottles and others wanted to bring in orange squash. These issues were raised by the children in the School Council. Now I buy bottles so that they can be sold in school, and the head teacher decided that only water could be drunk in the classrooms. Children are allowed to bring in squash or fruit juices with their packed lunch boxes.

One day a child in the School Council stood up and said that they weren't happy with the school dinners. This prompted lots of discussion, and the Council decided to carry out a survey across the school. It turned out that many children were unhappy. They thought that the meals were cold, they didn't like the choice and the daily menus didn't correspond to what the children were eating on a given day. So the children wrote letters to the caterers whilst I took the issue to the Healthy Schools Working Group and we sent a letter as well. One of the catering managers came to a School Council meeting and listened to the children's concerns. Although the children didn't get everything they wanted, they were pleased that they had been listened to. The menus began to correspond to the meals, and an inspector came to examine the temperature of the ovens in which we heated the school meals. This was an improvement, but very recently, we obtained new kitchen equipment and have now changed to a different provider of school meals.

Useful Information

Schools Council UK

The Schools Council UK provides training and resources for schools wishing to develop pupil participation and their citizenship programmes.

Schools Councils UK
Resources Department
57 Etchingham Park Road
London
N3 2EB

Tel. 020 8349 1917

www.schoolcouncils.org

Providing Emotional Support for Food and Body Image Problems

The following interviews were carried out with people who provide emotional, and sometimes medical or social, support to children. They can be a very important source of help to a school that has a concern about a child's eating.

The Family Liaison Officer

Family liaison officers were introduced into the most deprived areas of Kent with funding from the Children's Fund. Kerry Collins and Jackie Moull are family liaison officers in different schools and each explains their role in terms of bringing school, families and community services together to best meet the needs of children. Although both are directly involved with children's eating through breakfast clubs and fruit schemes, they both see these as part of a much more important objective, that is to raise children's self-esteem and confidence, and to encourage their social skills. For many children, family liaison officers act as their first line of pastoral support.

Schools' Counselling Service

For children needing more specialist services for emotional health problems, such as eating distress, an eating disorder, being bullied or underlying family problems, the Schools' Counselling Service can help. In Kent, the service extends to primary schools. Brian Molloy, the director of the Schools' Counselling Service in East Kent, has provided details of the information that is distributed to local schools.

The School Nurse

Children might require the emotional, medical or educational support that can be provided by the School Nursing Service. Chris Beer, Fiona Annis and Carol Boxall explain the wide range of services which school nurses provide for children in schools.

The Community Paediatrician

Dr Liz Tanner is a community paediatrician who meets children with eating problems, such as eating disorders and obesity, regularly. She explains how children with eating problems are medically assessed and treated, along with some of the current challenges to providing good health care in this field. Liz also reflects on her own views about why children develop and maintain such problems.

The Family Liaison Officer

The role of the family liaison officer can be very broad, so two interviews with family liaison officers in Kent were undertaken.

Kerry Collins
Family Liaison Officer

Family liaison officers (FLO's) began to work with children and families about eight years ago, and were funded by social services and education. More recently Kent received money from the Children's Fund money to support family liaison officers being introduced into the 75 most deprived wards in Kent. This was based on figures such as the number of children having free school meals, the number living in council homes the numbers of single mothers and so forth. However, the funding is for a set period of time, and the role of family liaison officers is being evaluated to see whether the initiative will be spread nationwide.

Our job is to provide support to children and families who may be experiencing difficulties. We work in the schools, and try to pick up issues early in order to prevent them from becoming problems. Our roles might be very different according to the schools in which we are based. It can cover a multitude of things, and no two days are the same. Some examples are being involved in first aid, lunch time groups, storytelling, drama, anger management, fruit tuck shops, water in schools and healthy lunch boxes. FLO's will often work with other statutory agencies such as school nurses, social services and housing services, and with non-statutory agencies such as counselling services, Home Start and the Citizens Advice Bureau.

How are you selected?

Family liaison officers are selected on the basis of experience. They have often worked within health-related or school settings, and usually have families themselves. It's helpful to have an education background, but it's more important to have had experience with children, as a FLO spends a lot of time with children. It's important to have empathy with people, and you need the right FLO with the right head teacher with the right school. These things are more important than formal qualifications. All FLO's have induction training which covers child protection, health, safety and so forth.

How can you help?

I spend a lot of my time in the playground talking to parents. They find me and off-load. A big part of my role is sign-posting them to where they can get help. It isn't for me to take their troubles on board and sort them out, it is about finding the right person who can help, or empowering them to help themselves. Sometimes just by talking things through, they find the confidence to go and sort it out themselves. They come back and say, "I did that. It worked." This spreads, by word of mouth, around the playground. They get to know that I could be a good person to talk to. Equally people who are not confident about the school sometimes ask me to go with them when they need to talk to a teacher.

There is a fair amount of pastoral care with children in school as a way of trying to cut down school exclusions, and increase attendance. Some FLO's do the first role call, to make sure the children are in school, and if they're not they follow it up with parents. Sometimes, just the fact that someone has noticed, will prompt a parent to get the child to school on time.

Some FLO's do Circle Time, anger management and emotional literacy work with small groups of up to ten children. It will depend on their background and experience, and also the needs of the schools and the school philosophy.

How can you contribute to healthier eating?

The breakfast club has been a fantastic success here. I did the background research and set it up. We have 32 children a day coming for breakfast and, sadly, a waiting list because we can't accommodate more than 32. We've really seen some positive developments in children because of the breakfast club. We had one child, who was in Year 6 last year, who had very low self-esteem. By coming to breakfast club he not only got a breakfast, which he wasn't having before because he wasn't getting out of bed early enough, but he was mixing with younger children which boosted his own self-esteem. I have also introduced fruit in the morning for the reception class, water bottles into other classes, and water coolers into the school. I'm pleased with these developments because they are sustainable, and are here to stay.

It has taken time to build up the relationships with the people, school and the children, but now I really feel that I am there for the families, and they seem to look forward to seeing me. I don't stand on my own in the playground that's for sure!

Jackie Moull
Family Liaison Officer

One of my main duties is to manage the Breakfast Club where the children have cereals, fruit juice, crumpets, fresh fruit and toast, and then we have a games trolley containing various books and activities which the children can use before going in the playground. I organise the fruit stall at break time, and I run a second hand uniform stall on a Friday. This relies on parents sending in uniforms that the children have outgrown or no longer need. I take them home and wash them and do minor repairs. I price them up, and nothing is more than £2.50. I arrange a trip a term for parents and children. This isn't educational in a traditional sense, for example it could be a trip to the pantomime or zoo. Some families have never been in a theatre, some don't know what a pantomime is. They pay a minimum charge and I make all the arrangements. They really enjoy it. It's quite moving really, because you know you are doing something that these parents wouldn't think of doing.

I also run an ADHD (Attention Deficit Hyperactivity Disorder) and Challenging Behaviour Support Group. It began because we have several children who have been statemented due to ADHD, and we have several children who have not been statemented, but who are clearly bordering on ADHD. The parents were definitely needing some kind of support. It seems the local clinic just didn't have the manpower or time to devote to parents as well as the children. So I started one up, and invited parents from other schools, through the other family liaison officers at other schools. I try to get a different speaker each month. They could be speaking about anything that is related to challenging behaviour, perhaps causing a disturbance in the family, such as asthma, incontinence or epilepsy. A recent speaker came from Partnership with Parents, a group that supports parents about school matters and will act as mediators. I had an educational psychologist one month, which was like striking gold for these parents. The parents found her very useful. We do a lot of work around diet, and we have a dietitian coming soon. Foods like cheese, chocolate, some additives and excessive sugar are the key culprits. A lot of these children have packed lunches, but we also work with the catering company who try not to include additives in the school meals. They also have a list of children who are affected by certain foods.

I also run a lunchtime club for children who have problems socialising in the playground. These are children who find it difficult when there are a lot of people around, and they are left to amuse themselves. They aren't able to do this. So at the lunchtime club we play games such as lego, building bricks and KNEX. I sit with them. I have a core group, and then other children choose to join us every now and then.

All these activities are about someone taking an interest in the children. A lot of them don't get much attention at home. They come to school, and school is the one stable factor in their lives. A lot of them are from broken homes, with little stability, or structure. They are so needy, and needing affection. Some of them are only too eager to give affection to anyone who pays them any kind of attention. Frequently children run up to me and give me a big hug, no matter what they are doing. The emotional side is very important for these children.

Useful Information

The Children's Fund

The Children's Fund is a programme within the Government's Children, Young People and Families Directorate (formerly the Children's and Young People's Unit). It is targeted at 5 to 13 year olds and supports initiatives designed to poverty and social exclusion amongst the young.

The Children's and Young People's Unit has a web site www.allchildrenni.gov.uk Their contact telephone number is 0870 000 2288.

Department for Education and Skills

The Children and Families Directorate web site contains a wide range of key Government documents relating to children's welfare (www.dfes.gov.uk/childrenandfamilies).

ADHD

The National Institute of Clinical Excellence has published advice about ADHD for health professionals.

NICE (2000) *Guidance on the Use of Methylphenidate (Ritalin, Equasym) for Attention Deficit Hyperactivity Disorder (ADHD) in Childhood*, London.

(www.nice.org.uk/article.asp?a=11667) See Appendix C: Patient Information

Available from:

NICE
MidCity Place
High Holborn
London
WC1V 6NA

www.nice.org.uk

Tel. 0541 555 455 and quote reference number 22593

Antidote

Antidote works towards a vision of an emotionally literate society. They carry out research, conferences, training and consultancy.

Antidote: Campaign for Emotional Literacy
Cityside House
3rd Floor (c/o Happy Computers)
40 Adler Street
London
E1 1EE

Tel. 020 7247 3355

www.antidote.org.uk

Useful book

Weare, K. (2000) *Promoting Mental, Emotional and Social Health. A Whole School Approach*, Routledge.

Schools' Counselling Service

Brian Molloy
Director, Schools' Counselling Service

The Schools' Counselling Service was established in East Kent in 1989 to meet the need for easy access to counselling support for students in school. The counsellors are qualified and police-checked. Their professional management and supervision is funded by the Primary Care Trust, who also pay for some of the counselling in schools. Some schools pay for the time that the counsellor is working with them. The Service also has the support of the Local Education Authority and Social Services.

In accordance with the British Association for Counselling and Psychotherapy guidelines, the overall aim of counselling is to provide an opportunity for the young person to work towards living in a way that he or she perceives as more satisfying or resourceful. The objective of a counselling relationship will vary according to the young person's needs. Counselling may be concerned with developmental issues, addressing and resolving specific problems, making decisions, coping with crisis, developing personal insight and knowledge, working through feelings of inner conflict, or improving relationships with others. The counsellor's role is to facilitate the young person's work in ways that respect the young person's values, personal resources and capacity for choice within his or her cultural context. Counselling involves a deliberately undertaken contract with clearly agreed boundaries and commitment to privacy and confidentiality. It requires explicit and informed consent according to age criteria agreed by the Service.

School counsellors might help children with a wide range of issues including stress, family difficulties, the loss of a significant family member or close friend, the loss associated with divorce, difficulties with peer relationships such as bullying, abuse, issues associated with drugs and eating problems.

Before making a referral, schools are asked to consider the following six points:

1. Before referring a student you should check out their commitment to engage in counselling. Also be mindful that this is a voluntary activity, although students sometimes use the service as part of a contract with the school to avoid exclusion.

2. The counsellor will always be pleased to discuss a referral with you beforehand if you have any concerns as to whether counselling is appropriate.

3. It is preferable that all students under 16 years of age have a parent or carer's consent to attend counselling. It is mandatory for students under 14 years of age.

4. Counsellors normally see the young person on a weekly basis, for an average of about six hours. Each counselling session is usually of 30 minutes duration. The counsellors are encouraged to work in focused and creative ways to maximise the effectiveness of the process.

5. Brief notes of the work with each student are kept. These are confidential to the counsellor and student.

6. Counsellors need to know if there are child protection issues or other agencies involved.

Useful Information

British Association for Counselling and Psychotherapy

The British Association for Counselling and Psychotherapy is the leading professional body for counselling and psychotherapy in the UK. It is normally desirable that practitioners are BACP registered.

British Association for Counselling and Psychotherapy
BACP House
35-37 Albert Street
Rugby
Warwickshire
CV21 2SG

Tel. 0870 443 5252

www.bacp.co.uk

ChildLine

www.childline.org.uk

ChildLine is the UK's free help line for children in distress. Through ChildLine in Partnership with Schools (CHIPS) ChildLine will provide schools with resources, information and run workshops. Offices are based around the UK with individual telephone numbers (see www.childline.org.uk/Contactus.asp).

Children's 24 hour Help Line Tel. 0800 1111

ChildLine's web site about children's eating problems can be accessed: www.childline.org.uk/eatingproblems.asp

National Centre for Eating Disorders

The National Centre for Eating Disorders carries out training for professionals, an information service, through its web site, and counselling.

National Centre for Eating Disorders
54 New Road
Esher
Surrey
KT10 9NU

Tel. 01372 469493

www.eating-disorders.org.uk

Eating Disorders Association

The Eating Disorders Association (EDS) provides information, help and support for people across the UK whose lives are affected by eating disorders. They aim to influence understanding and policy. Their web page, designed for young people to use, can be found: www.edauk.com/young_home.htm.

Eating Disorders Association
103 Prince of Wales Road
Norwich
NR1 1DW

Tel. 0870 770 3256

www.edauk.com

The School Nurse

Chris Beer, School Nurse Team Leader
Fiona Annis, School Nurse Team Leader
Carol Boxall, School Nurse, Adolescent Lead

What is a school nurse?

School nurses are registered general nurses, some are registered children's nurses who have had some community experience, and some are also family planning trained. Others will have undertaken the degree level specialist qualification in school nursing. School nursing is multi-tasked, and although the work is generic most school nurses have expertise in particular areas of practice. For example some specialise in asthma, enuresis, special needs, behavioural issues, adolescence and so forth. The aim of school nursing is to improve the health of future generations. We help ensure that children achieve their full potential. We are a confidential, universal service with open access to families and other agencies. It is also about being able to identify heath issues and to work with other services such as Sure Start, the police, Children's Fund, Social Services, Home Start, County Council and Family Planning.

How are children referred to you?

All schools have a school nursing team. Children might refer themselves or they might be referred by GPs, parents, social services, education indeed anybody. Once a child has been referred to the team, we allocate the most appropriately trained school nurse to that child.

What is a typical day for a school nurse?

The range of work is huge. Some days we might be attending meetings, some days we are in schools seeing the kids on a one-to-one basis. We have days when we are in and out of social services, giving immunisations, carrying out health education in schools, or training teachers, dinner ladies or parents. Most schools have a service level agreement, approved by the governors and parents, which outlines the service the school wishes to have. We can organise 'exit' cards which allow pupils 'time out' to go to a quiet room for anger management, or 'exeat' cards to allow them to get to a clinic.

Can you give me some examples of how school nurses can help children in the context of eating and body image?

A nurse can support schools with health education. In fact we're all dealing with self-image all the time. When we're delivering lessons on sexually transmitted infections we would include self-image. You bring everything in because nothing stands alone. When we are doing vaccination sessions we're always discussing food. 'Have you had your breakfast? Why haven't you had your breakfast?' It might be linked to why someone is feeling faint. So as well as formal sessions, there is a lot of incidental education.

In one school we have been talking about healthy eating, and as a result the school has taken a look at their kitchens and re-jigged their menus. We work with Healthy Schools teams and help schools to meet their healthy eating targets. For example, we have helped to promote water and fruit in schools. Recently a child who saw a nurse on a one-to-one basis about an issue concerning school dinners was advised to take the issue to the School Council, who responded very positively. We often link children to dentists, community dietitians or community paediatricians.

On a one-to-one basis we see children who might be concerned about being overweight. Related to this they might be being bullied, have poor hygiene or have dental cavities. It might be that a child's behaviour has changed, they have become aggressive and they are not eating. Once you unpack the issues, the most common underlying factor is family breakdown. We see many children who are suffering because they aren't being allowed to see dad, or dad has a new girlfriend or mum has a new boyfriend. They can't talk to anyone, and these are huge issues for them. Different schools have different issues, family breakdown, eating disorders and self harm are often linked and are common amongst girls in high achieving academic schools.

What can you do?

We refer children to our local Child and Adolescent Mental Health Service, or the School Counselling Service. However, both organisations require parental consent and this can be difficult when children don't want to talk to their parents. Eating disorders are all to do with control, and needing to have control over what they tell, and do not tell, their parents is part of it. Even if consent is obtained, there can be a long waiting list to obtain the counselling or therapy they need, and in this time they are deteriorating both psychologically and physically. We end up referring them to a paediatrician for hospital admission. This is why we need to improve the care pathway in Kent, so that children can be picked up much sooner. In the meantime we offer solution focused brief therapy. We try to befriend and support the children, to be their listener, we need to allow them to off-load. They often feel that they can't do it anywhere else because they feel too ashamed and hurt.

What are your views about the issue of dieting and the school setting?

I don't think we should ever discuss it unless you are working on a one-to-one with a child who is overweight. It could become like auto-suggestion. One local school is known for having a size 8 club, and when you are dealing with that type of mentality you have to be very careful. We wouldn't talk about eating disorders. We discuss healthy eating and self-esteem, and explore people's perceptions of other people.

What kinds of lessons do you find work well?

Pass the parcel where children discuss an issue which is tucked into each layer, or a treasure bag from which children take out points for discussion. Passing round pictures of celebrities, perhaps some very thin and some a little overweight, and asking the children, "What's your impression of this person?" This gets them thinking and allows you to challenge them about why they make certain judgements about others based on appearance. In one school we asked the children to bring in magazines, which were cut up and made into a collage. This provoked interesting discussion. Painting, drawing and poetry are all good for drawing out their issues.

Useful Information

The role of the school nurse

The Department of Health define the role of today's school nurse in Department of Health (2001) *School Nurse Practice Development Resource Pack*, London. Available from www.publications.doh. gov.uk/cno/schoolnursedevpack.pdf.

The Community Practitioners' and Health Visitors' Association provides professional and educational support for school nurses. Their web site contains key information about school nursing including the National Strategy for School Nursing Practice which outlines the future public health role of school nurses. The CPHVA's web site is www.msfcphva.org/schoolnursing/snhome.html

The *National Service Framework for Children, Young People and Maternity Services* (Department of Health, 2004c) advocated the need for local primary care trusts to increase the capacity of the school nursing workforce in order to address the key public health issues, such as child obesity, outlined in the *Choosing Health* White Paper (Department of Health, 2004).

Children's Services

The Department of Health, in cooperation with the Department for Education and Skills, oversee all health and social care for children in England. Details about Children's Services are available at www.dh.gov.uk/PolicyAndGuidance/HealthAndSocialCareTopics/ChildrenServices/fs/en

Children First for Health

Children First for Health (www.childrenfirst.nhs.uk) is an international health website devised by children for children. It includes a wide range of information about 'your health, your hospital and your life', including understanding the body, staying in hospital and bullying.

The Community Paediatrician

Dr Liz Tanner
Community Paediatrician

What is the role of a community paediatrician?

Community paediatricians qualify as doctors, then go onto a paediatric training scheme, usually working for three years in hospital, and then move into community paediatrics. After six months in the community there is the choice to train as a community paediatrician.

Before the NHS community paediatricians were the school doctors with designated schools. Now we take referrals of children who have developmental issues, neuro-pathology, behavioural disorders such as ADHD etc., so we don't routinely see 'well' children in the way we used to, and no longer do the screening in schools.

We are part of a multi-agency service working closely with education, social services, Child and Adolescent Mental Health Services (CAHMS) etc. My particular role is to act as the 'adolescent-lead' for children in both school and the community, for any children who need a physical assessment or treatment, rather than those who need emotional or psychological help from CAHMS. We sometimes do joint assessments, and this is now the proposed way forward.

How can you help with young people who have problems around eating?

With respect to eating disorders, I normally receive referrals from the GPs, teachers such as the Special Educational Needs Coordinators or Deputy Heads, parents or, most often, school nurses. If the issues cannot be resolved by the school, school nurse or counselling service, and there is much concern about behaviour and weight, I will see them quite intensively, normally in the community clinic at the local health centre. I carry out a physical examination, usually with a parent there, or at least with parental consent. Usually the individual will be referred on to CAHMS, and I continue to see them regularly to monitor their physical progress through blood tests etc. We can coordinate the treatment on this out-patient basis. Our aim is to provide a prevention service, to avoid a crisis, however, what tends to happen is that they are referred too late and then they have to have a hospital admission.

In this part of Kent we are trying to set up a care pathway whereby referrals go to a single point of entry. So that any child in the area with signs of an eating disorder is referred to myself, the community paediatrician, to have joint assessment with someone from CAHMS. Having decided on the severity of the situation there would be three routes. 1. Continue to see a school counsellor or school nurse and myself. 2. Refer to CAHMS and be seen within days. 3. Admitted to hospital. This process differs in other parts of the country, for example, the CAHMS team can be the first point of entry. However, to set up this pathway requires funding and support.

What are some of the key challenges in this field?

Some of the problems we encounter are that some GPs refer straight to hospital paediatrics and more people need to be aware that the community paediatrician might be the better point of entry so that CAHMS and myself can work together at an earlier stage.

Related to this is the problem of gaining accurate data. I have been referred 25 children with newly diagnosed eating disorders in the last year, many of whom were quite severe. This is well above the national average. We think CAHMS have had eight new cases. We think we are missing a lot because we don't know how many were directly referred to hospital paediatrics. Another problem can be long waiting lists to be seen by CAHMS teams.

What advice can you give to others who are working with young people?

Children with eating disorders are very well aware of healthy eating. The more you tell them about healthy eating, the worse they can get. They know more about calories than anyone. One of our problems is that we have a nation of obese people, including children, whilst we also have this minority who have eating disorders. If you go into schools and talk about the signs and symptoms of eating disorders, it can make it worse, but talking about social problems helps. It's a fine line we tread. As the majority of people have a problem with eating too much and being overweight, they do need to know about healthy eating.

I see children and teenagers who are overweight too, and that's the other side of the coin. Very often they have an eating disorder anyway – bingeing. They know what is healthy, but they choose not to follow it or find they can't. This isn't easy to deal with because often it is a family issue and the family is overweight. The best way of treating them is to raise their self-esteem. With so many young people, whether they are overweight or self-harmers, it is often a self-esteem issue on the whole, for both girls and boys. Body awareness issues among boys is an increasing problem. If their self-esteem is raised in whatever way, they often do very well, particularly if you are able to address family issues as well. Where we have had great success has been with those kids who have been picked up early, where you recognise what the emotional issues are and they get into family therapy or onto a self-esteem programme. This might be at CAHMS, but sometimes it is self-initiated. If you pick them up early you can work with them, and the more success you have.

I think that the issues are often about the journey into adolescence, which is getting younger and younger. It is important for parents to understand how to deal with children who are going through early adolescence. Parenting classes would be great, such as understanding children's issues, and how not to worry kids too much, and how parents should avoid being over-protective in many ways.

Useful Information

Eating Disorders

The National Institute of Clinical Excellence has published a series of guidelines for the management of eating disorders. The most useful for school personnel and parents are:

NICE (2004) *Eating Disorders: Anorexia Nervosa, Bulimia Nervosa and Related Eating Disorders. Understanding NICE Guidance: A Guide for People, their Advocates and Carers and The Public*, London ISBN 1842574973

and

NICE (2004) *Quick Reference Guide. Eating Disorders. Core Interventions in The Treatment and Management of Anorexia Nervosa, Bulimia Nervosa and Related Eating Disorders. Clinical Guideline 9*, London.

Both available from:

NICE
MidCity Place
High Holborn
London
WC1V 6NA

www.nice.org.uk

or the NHS Response Line Tel. 0870 1555455 and ask for Ref No.NO407 (English) or N0408 (English and Welsh).

The Association for the Study of Obesity (ASO)

The Association for the Study of Obesity (ASO) has an excellent web site providing useful information about recent research into the causes, consequences, treatment and prevention of obesity.

ASO
Administrative Officer
20 Brook Meadow Close
Woodford Green
Essex
IG8 9NR

www.aso.org.uk

The Obesity Awareness and Solutions Trust (TOAST)

TOAST is a charity that works for the prevention and management of obesity in the UK.

TOAST
PO Box 6430
Harlow
Essex
CM18 7TT
Tel. 01279 866010

www.toast-uk.org.uk

Providing Education about Healthier Eating

The following interviews illustrate a range of educational support which is available for both staff and pupils, who want to achieve healthier eating in their schools.

Healthy Eating within the Healthy Schools Programme

Jennifer Holland is the coordinator for the East Kent Healthy Schools Programme, within the Kent Health and Education Partnership. Jennifer explains how she set up a Healthy Eating Strategy Group which brought together expertise from schools and the wider community to address healthy eating within the Healthy School Programme. She outlines how that expertise was disseminated throughout Kent, and how the East Kent Healthy Schools team support schools in their area.

The Hydrate Project

Paula Gill is a community worker who led a project to promote the drinking of water among primary school pupils. The Hydrate Project was a research exercise led by pupils with educational and emotional difficulties, working with the local community. It not only achieved greater awareness of the importance of drinking water throughout the school, but had some marked social and emotional benefits for the pupils.

The School Meal Nutritionist

Carla Maurici is a nutritionist working for a supplier of school meals. She checks the nutrient content of the meals and provides nutrition education for staff and pupils in schools. Schools might find nutritionists working for their own school meal provider to be a very useful source of information and resources, provided the school is satisfied that they are providing impartial advice.

The Community Dental Service

Camilla Joarder is the senior dental health officer for the East Kent Community Dental Service. She works as a dentist and coordinates dental health promotion work in her area, producing dental health information and contributing to Healthy Schools conferences.

The Dental Therapist

Sue Scrivens is an experienced dental therapist who shares her ideas for making dental education fun and meaningful for primary school children.

The Community Dietitian

Abi Mogridge is a community dietitian who explains how community dietitians undertake both clinical and educational work. Many community dietitians are playing an increasing role in promoting healthy eating in schools and at home.

Healthy Eating Within the Healthy Schools Programme

Jennifer Holland
Healthy Schools Programme Coordinator

The National Healthy Schools Standard was set up in 1999. In Kent it was decided that someone should take a lead on each of the eight themes of the Standard on behalf of the whole of Kent (The Kent Health and Education Partnership). My previous work had been carrying out research into health promoting schools across Europe and ten years' experience of teaching home economics, catering and food technology in schools.

One of my first tasks was to set up a Healthy Eating Strategy Group which could utilise local expertise and support schools in developing healthier eating. The group includes a dental officer, a community dietitian, teachers, the person from the County Council responsible for school meals, a school milk project facilitator and so forth. Together they have a wide range of resources, expertise and practical experience to contribute. A good example of this occurred recently when we were discussing the presence of a coke vending machine in one school, and the dental officer told us that she knew the school was among those who had the highest incidence of dental caries in East Kent. So we instantly had access to some useful evidence to inform negotiations with schools. My role is to encourage schools to consult with their communities and to identify their own needs. If they have needs around healthy eating I, along with the help of the Strategy Group, try to help.

Initially we ran a training event, as a large conference, to raise the agenda of healthy eating in schools across Kent. Many representatives from the schools who had expressed an interest in doing something about healthy eating came along, and I think we were very successful in raising their awareness about the importance and breadth of healthy eating in schools. After this, I worked with the schools to help them to identify targets. For many schools, the setting up of a breakfast club was their first target. So I applied for funding from the Children's Fund to support the setting up of the breakfast clubs in these schools, and further funding to support the post of a breakfast club coordinator for two years. She helped with planning, monitoring and training, and although the funding has just finished, the breakfast clubs are all established and running successfully.

Next, the Strategy Group and I identified the need to encourage children in schools to eat more fruit. I was lucky enough to find a packer in Canterbury who was willing to supply free fruit to schools in east and mid Kent for one term only. I developed some guidance for the schools that sold the fruit at ten pence per item at break time. In this way, the schools were able to raise some money that was used the following term to help establish their own fruit tuck shops based on fruit that they purchased. A number of schools got going in this way, and we now have a large number of schools in Kent operating fruit tuck shops because the 'word has spread' and schools have supported one another. It is often through achieving success in one aspect of healthy eating, such as setting up a breakfast club or a fruit tuck shop, that a school becomes involved in other aspects of the Healthy Schools Programme and decide to commit to every area of the Programme.

Our second conference for schools across Kent focussed on how to develop a whole-school food policy. We included workshops which concentrated on the curriculum and teaching at different key stages, and workshops for school caterers. The third conference, which we are currently organising, will be about taking healthy eating beyond the classroom. So it will include growing food, composting, packed lunches and links to physical activity. We are inviting a catering lecturer with substantial experience to come and do a cookery demonstration. He is being asked to cook an acceptable, interesting and healthy meal, using some organic produce, on the budget that is allocated to a school meal.

My work also brings me into direct contact with many schools. On the basis of local social and educational data, we target schools for which there is evidence of significant need and offer our support. However, any school can request a healthy schools specialist, from their local health promotion unit, to visit them. If the school is not already part of a local Healthy Schools Programme, I would normally ask the school whether they would like to become involved. If they agree, they are asked to undergo a process of self-review using an evaluation tool. On the basis of the results, I work with the person who is designated as the healthy schools coordinator to set targets for health improvement. Thereafter we have regular review meetings and occasionally I attend the school's Healthy School Working Group. The Healthy Schools Programme is about trying to ensure that every aspect of the school lends support to what is being taught in the classroom so, for example, I've developed a course about healthy eating for parents, which I have run in school kitchens. There is also a lot of interest in growing fruit and vegetables, so I am working with some schools to see how we can develop school gardens. Currently, I'm trying to access funding to support and expand both of these initiatives.

One challenge that I face is getting more schools to move forward from embracing one strategy, such as setting up a breakfast club, to embracing a whole-school approach to health improvement. The evidence shows that it is only if the whole school is working towards promoting healthier eating that positive dietary change happens, and this not only applies to healthy eating but to improving other aspects of health also. So the key is to capitalise on one initiative and keep the school's impetus going towards a whole-school approach, and then onwards towards meeting the criteria which means they can be called a Healthy School.

Useful Information

Wired for Health

www.wiredforhealth.gov.uk

The Wired for Health web site provides a comprehensive guide to all aspects of health within the context of the national curriculum and the National Healthy Schools Programme.

Kent Healthy Schools

www.kenthealthyschools.org

The Kent Healthy Schools web site contains useful information for pupils, parents and teachers as well as key contacts and useful web sites.

British Nutrition Foundation

The British Nutrition Foundation (BNF) is a charitable organisation that promotes the nutritional wellbeing of society through disseminating impartial, scientifically based, nutritional advice. The BNF works with academic and research institutes, the professions, the food industry, educators and the government. Their comprehensive and extensive resources for schools are discussed in the Education section of their web site (www.nutrition.org.uk).

British Nutrition Foundation
High Holborn House
52-54 High Holborn
London
WC1V 6RQ
Tel. 020 7404 6504

www.nutrition.org.uk

Food Standards Agency

The Food Standards Agency is an independent food safety watchdog set up by an Act of Parliament in 2000 to protect the public's health and consumer interests in relation to food. For information on healthy eating see www.eatwell.gov.uk.

Their Diet and Health web pages include a number of initiatives related to healthier eating in schools (www.food.gov.uk/healthiereating)

A useful publication is *School-based Food Initiatives* available at www.food.gov.uk/multimedia/pdfs/bookmarknut.pdf

Food Standards Agency
Aviation House
125 Kingsway
London
WC2B 6NH
Tel. 020 7276 8000

www.food.gov.uk

Sustain

Sustain is a charity representing over 100 national public interest organisations, all working towards better food and farming. It produces a wide range of publications and has a very informative web site. See in particular the Campaign for the Children's Food Bill and Grab 5.

SUSTAIN
94 White Lion Street
London
N1 9PF
Tel. 020 7837 1228

www.sustainweb.org

Health Education Trust

The Health Education Trust is a UK registered charity, formed to promote the development of health education for young people in the UK. It has carried out extensive work to promote healthier eating in schools, including pioneering School Nutrition Action Groups and setting up a database for school catering.

Health Education Trust
18 High Street
Broom
Alcester
Warwickshire
B50 4HJ

www.healthedtrust.com

The Food Commission

The Food Commission describes itself as the leading consumer watchdog on food issues. It campaigns for safer food and has carried out a range of research around children's food. Its publications include:

- *Children's Food*

- *Food Labelling*

- *Food Additives*

- *The Nursery Food Book*

- *The Food our Children Eat*

- *The Chips are Down* (in cooperation with the Health Education Trust).

The Food Commission wrote its own Children's Nutrition Action Plan in 2001.

The Food Commission
94 White Lion Street
London N1 9PF

www.foodcomm.org.uk

The Hydrate Project

Paula Gill
Community Networker

I worked as a registered nurse with children who have learning disabilities, and set up a project for young carers before I came here to the Healthy Living Network. I am employed as a community networker, with a remit to focus on children and families, by the Council for Voluntary Service who manage Project Sunlight. Project Sunlight is a Healthy Living Network for Medway, and my job is to use holistic approaches to tackle health inequalities through networking and supporting the setting up of projects that will have a positive impact on health. The Hydrate Project was one of these projects. Much of my work is about empowering children. I have a passion for children's rights and believe that working with children directly is the way to improve their lifestyle. Thereafter I hope that this will filter through to the families and extended families.

How did the Hydrate Project begin?

The Hydrate Project began when I did some research and found out that many children are dehydrated in schools, and that they should be drinking six to eight glasses of water a day to prevent symptoms such as headaches, poor concentration, bad breath, heat intolerance, poor concentration and lethargy. Through being a member of the local healthy schools steering group I found a primary school that was interested in a water project, and allowed me access to a Year 6 class. The school served two local refuges and the local army barracks, so there was a lot of movement of children. All the children in the class were diagnosed as having educational and emotional difficulties, their academic achievement was poor and at least two of the children were unable to read. There was a high risk of these children being excluded once they moved to secondary school. The Hydrate Project was a way of building something positive into the school, particularly for children for whom school was not a good place to be, whilst also improving the potential for health.

There were three parts to the Project, the research, a whole-school poster competition and a school assembly. I started with the idea for the research. I wanted the project to be very participatory, and for the children to carry out research within the school. So initially a letter of explanation was sent to the families of the whole school, because all the children were going to be involved and photographs were going to be taken. Secondly, as this wasn't strictly within the national curriculum, a separate letter was sent to the families of the Year 6 class in order to gain parental consent for the children to take part in the project. This was the first difficult hurdle as we had considerable problems ensuring that the children took the letter home, that it was read and signed and brought back again. The school thought that this might be because many letters from school to these families had contained negative information in the past, and perhaps families had just stopped reading letters. Eventually ten, out of the 23 children in the class, came back with parental consent, and those ten became the researchers. The aim of the project was to raise awareness and increase the consumption of tap water.

The first stage was to teach the Year 6 class about water, particularly focusing on tap water. Once they had grasped the benefits of drinking more water and the signs and symptoms of dehydration, the children were asked to think about what kind of questions might go into a questionnaire. We ended up with about 13 possible questions. On the basis of these, the ten children agreed on four questions such as, "How many glasses of water do you drink in a day?" and, "How many glasses of water should you drink in a day?" They went on to design and produce the final questionnaire on the computer that helped them to practise skills around design and working together as a group. Each of the ten children asked five children in the school to complete their questionnaire, so they had answers from 50 completed questionnaires to collate.

Meanwhile two other initiatives were ongoing. Southern Water supported a school poster competition. This came about because Southern Water didn't have any child-friendly literature, and they suggested that the winning poster might be used by their publicity department. Concurrently a Project Sunlight volunteer, with experience of working with children in youth theatre, worked with the ten children to put on a school assembly about the reasons for drinking water. That was fantastic, and a really major achievement for children who would never have dreamt of presenting to the whole school. Southern Water donated three prizes of £25 gift vouchers for the best posters, which were given out at that assembly, and re-usable water bottles to each child in the school.

Following the assembly the ten children continued with their research. Each child, armed with another five questionnaires, went into classrooms and asked the teachers if anyone would be willing to fill in their questionnaires for them. In this way they were learning to take responsibility, something that they much needed in readiness for going to secondary school. As the research was going on at the same time as the assembly and the posters, the result was that children throughout the school were talking about water. This resulted in the ten children being made to feel increasingly important, and their self-esteem and confidence rose. The ten children collated the findings from the second round of research, and the results showed that there had been an increase in both awareness and the consumption of tap water. Each of the ten children received a certificate and a gift voucher from Medway Health Promotion.

Can you tell me some of the emotional and social benefits of the Hydrate Project?

Initially the children were difficult to manage. For example, on my first visit a child got up and hit another child across the head. That's the kind of immediate anger that some of the children were dealing with. I went into the school once a week for six months, and directly worked with the children for 40 minutes in their PSHE lesson. The class teacher was very supportive, but the practical on-going encouragement came from the pastoral assistant. I put a lot of emphasis on choice, they didn't have to do this. In fact one child withdrew, which was fine, and it confirmed to the others that what I was saying about choice was true. I used lots of positive reinforcement. Some children found it difficult to accept praise, or seemed surprised that they had achieved something that had been noted by others. I monitored how the group was feeling throughout the project by asking the children to do things like complete little questionnaires using smiley faces. As the project progressed the behaviour in the sessions improved, they were much better at negotiation and working with each other. Some smiled more easily in response to praise, which suggested to me that they had an increased belief in themselves. They were clearly very proud of their achievements.

What advice would you give to a school that wanted to carry out a similar project?

It is a succinct piece of work with clear boundaries, so I think a number of people could work in partnership with a school and help. Local businesses often want to make stronger links to their local communities. A parent, the local volunteer bureau or a student might help, even if it is just helping the children to collate or present their findings. Obviously police checks would have to be done. Our partners were Children's Fund Medway who funded the school pastoral assistant, Medway Healthy Schools, Medway Health Promotion Department and Southern Water. Now Medway Healthy Schools promote the Hydrate Project as a model for increasing water in schools.

Useful Information

SEBDA

SEBDA, the Social, Emotional and Behavioural Difficulties Association, aims to promote excellence in services for children who have emotional and behavioural difficulties, and to support those who work with them.

SEBDA
c/o Ted Cole
SEBDA Head Office

Church House
1 St Andrew's View
Penrith
Cumbria
CA10 7YF
Tel. 01768 210510

www.awcebd.co.uk

Mental Health Foundation

Bright Futures is a comprehensive and inspiring children's and young people's mental health programme including research, publications and advice.

The Mental Health Foundation
7th Floor
83 Victoria Street
London
SW1H OHW
Tel. 020 7802 0300

www.mentalhealth.org.uk

Water Education

Scottish Water have a useful education web site at www.scottishwater.co.uk/education.

Three Valleys Water's education pages are at www.3valleys.co.uk/education/index.shtml

The School Meal Nutritionist

Carla Maurici
Nutritionist

My role involves spending a great deal of time on school-related work, which includes ensuring that nutrition legislation is met, setting nutrition policy and carrying out nutrition education activities within schools. School menus are developed at a local level, according to regional preferences, and the nutrition department in which I work checks that they meet the Government's standards for school meals. We also check the nutrient content of primary school menus against the Caroline Walker Trust Guidelines, and work within nutrition policies that are based on recommendations from the British Nutrition Foundation and Anaphylaxis UK.

We currently cater for more than a thousand children with specific dietary requirements, from nut allergies to coeliac disease. All children referred to us with a special dietary requirement come via a medical referral, and we try to make dishes for them which are as similar as possible to the foods being eaten by their peers, though this is not always possible. We employ a nut-free policy in our primary schools, and insist that all children with nut allergies are referred to our nutrition department as a matter of safety.

Another part of my work is undertaking nutrition education in schools. I base teaching sessions around the Balance of Good Health, and try to get balanced eating messages across to the children in an age-appropriate and fun manner. One of the children's favourite messages from these sessions is, "No food is a bad food, but you can eat a bad diet!" This message reiterates to children that it is perfectly acceptable to eat their favourite foods as part of a balanced diet and that no food is prohibited.

As these workshops tend to be carried out throughout the day with different classes taking part at different times, I'm often able to share a school meal with the children. This is an excellent opportunity for me to demonstrate, in a practical way, balanced food choices to the children, through my own food choices and through the Initial Catering Services' Body Benefitter Cards. These are signs at service points that highlight the benefit of a particular food in the body, for example, foods rich in calcium have a sign reading, 'Feed your bones today'. The children tend to enjoy the meal experience and ask lots of questions, and sharing the meal with the children is also an excellent way of enabling them to develop other social skills around eating.

Our nutrition department has recently travelled around the UK obtaining children's feedback on new recipes. The most popular recipes have been recorded and will shortly be produced as a recipe booklet and made available to our cooks. Some are already appearing on our menus.

Useful Information

Initial Catering Services UK

Initial Catering Services has developed a range of resources for schools which include posters, a teachers' balanced eating teaching pack and an award-winning website www.coolmeals.co.uk.

The Nutrition Department Initial Catering Services Ltd
Bridge House
Mathisen Way
Colnbrook
Berkshire
SL3 0HH
Tel: 01753 561730

Food Allergies

Allergy UK is a charity committed to increasing awareness and understanding of allergies.

Allergy UK
No 3 White Oak Square
London Road
Swanley
Kent
BR8 7AG

www.allergyuk.org

The Community Dental Service

Camilla Joarder
Senior Dental Officer for Dental Health Promotion

Community dentists are dentists who have undertaken extra community vocational training to treat children and adults with special needs and those with phobias. In addition, a senior dental officer for health promotion will usually have a postgraduate diploma or masters in health promotion.

I am accountable to the director of dental services in this area. I spend three days a week on clinical work and two days on health promotion. My health promotion work encompasses anything to do with oral health promotion in this area. I facilitate the work of the dental therapists, who go into schools, playgroups and so forth. We have quarterly meetings and my colleagues across the southeast and I organise an annual conference for them and other health promoters. The job is very much responding to requests in the community, from Age Concern to Sure Start, although sometimes I am more proactive. I am sometimes invited to do some teaching for health professionals such as health visitors, school nurses, district nurses and midwives, and together with the dental therapists I produce dental health resources for various audiences. My work with the Healthy Schools Healthy Eating team has included writing a page about sport drinks and wearing gum shields for their web pages and newsletters, and contributing to their conferences for local schools. If schools would like the community dental service to work with them in promoting dental health, they should initially phone their local dental officer for health promotion. In the meantime, some of the companies, such as Colgate, produce some good educational materials.

Useful Information

Colgate-Palmolive (UK) Ltd

The Colgate Kids web site is designed for parents, teachers and children.

Colgate-Palmolive (UK) Ltd
Guildford Business Park
Middleton Road
Guildford
Surrey
GU2 8JZ

www.colgate.co.uk

Oral B

Oral B is part of the Gillette company based in the USA. Their Oral B Learning Centre web site includes Teaching Tools (for teachers) www.oralb.com/learningcenter

Oral B
Gillette Group UK Ltd
Gillette Corner
Great West Road
Isleworth
Middlesex TW7 5NP

Tel. 020 83268862

The Dental Therapist

Sue Scrivens
Dental Therapist

The role of the dental therapist is to improve dental health within the community. Usually people enter dental therapy having worked as a dental hygienist or dental nurse. Some Dental Schools offer the Diploma in Dental Therapy which usually covers the dual qualification of being both a hygienist and therapist. Dental therapists have a limited clinical role carrying out fillings, extractions and injections, and carry out dental health education within settings such as play groups, schools, post-natal groups and residential homes for the elderly.

What are the challenges faced by dental therapists?

The main challenge is that the people to whom you would most like to speak are those who are the most difficult to reach. This is why dental health education in schools is so good. You have an almost captive audience, whereas in other settings people are there because they are already motivated and choose to be there. In school you can reach almost everyone. However, sometimes you would like to speak to parents too, and you can't access them.

How often do you visit schools?

I link with 90 infant and primary schools and I try to get to each one once every 12 to 18 months. I aim to speak to all Reception and Year 1 children, and to nine to ten year olds in Key Stage 2, so that each child sees me twice during their time at primary school. On the basis of school dental screening, carried out by dental surgeons, we obtain 'Decayed, Missing, Filled (DMF)' figures and can identify schools where there is greater need for extra visits. Sometimes teachers phone me, particularly if they are covering 'my body' or 'healthy eating', or I will approach the school.

How do you like to teach children at Key Stage 2 about dental care?

I usually begin by explaining the basic decay process. I write and draw this on the board using different colours. For example, I might discuss foods that contain sugar. I will write the words and draw a can of coke, cakes and ice cream. I think that presenting the information visually helps the children to remember. I make up little pictures of cartoon men as bacteria. I might talk about sugar in general, how sugar is in our foods, how we read labels on packaging, how to find out if food has sugar, different sorts of sugars and how to find out how much sugar is in something. I demonstrate this by putting different teaspoons of sugar into a pot, according to different products that I show them.

I ask the children for their ideas about what we should do about sugar and tooth decay. Of course someone will always say, "Don't eat sugar," then someone might say, "Cut down." I say that's a good idea and ask them to think about how we might cut down. I listen to their ideas and we discuss them. We will usually discuss trying to cut down on sugar in tea and coffee, diet soft drinks and healthier alternatives such as milk. Fruit and vegetables come into this discussion: why we should eat these and how we can make healthier packed lunches.

Then I return to bacteria and we talk about how we have bacteria in our bodies and bacteria in our mouths that leads us to the build up of plaque. We consider what we can do about this, and inevitably begin to consider tooth brushing and things that we can all do on an everyday basis. Then we might talk about visiting the dentist and how the dentist is not just looking for bad teeth, he or she is also looking at the health of our gums and whether our teeth are straight.

After this structured session, I like to have a much more open period when the children can ask me anything at all about teeth. Children might ask about their teeth, animal teeth, grandma's teeth, herbivores, carnivores and so forth. I enjoy this and so do the children. I then encourage the teaching staff to build on this work.

I make my own resources, although it is possible to obtain some items such as large teeth through school education suppliers. A random sample of schools is sent a questionnaire on a regular basis, so that we dental therapists can evaluate our work.

What would be your 'top tips' for encouraging good dental care for Key Stage 2 children?

"Many children really enjoy reading labels. They are often aware of fat and salt, and then I come along and we look at sugar. So I would say encourage the children to read the labels so that they can find out for themselves what is in their food, and this gives them a sense of achievement.

If we are talking about cutting down on sugar, I recommend that they do this in stages, from two teaspoons of sugar in tea to one, and then to a half and then a quarter. That's a much easier process than just stopping. I also encourage them to set targets such as, "I'm going to be taking one teaspoon of sugar by Christmas, and a half by Easter."

I always appreciate the teacher staying to listen to my sessions. I think that if the teacher stays it sends a message to the children that the teacher thinks my session is important, and also the teacher is able to build on the contributions made by both myself and the children.

Useful Information

British Association of Dental Therapists

The British Association of Dental Therapists supports the profession, and provides information to the public about the role of a dental therapist.

British Association of Dental Therapists

Tel. 0118 947 9399

www.badt.org.uk

British Dental Health Foundation

The British Dental Health Foundation is an oral health charity providing information and support to both professionals and the public. Through the professional area of their web site they produce a range of educational resources.

British Dental Health Foundation
Smile House
2 East Union Street
Rugby
Warwickshire
CV22 6AJ
Tel. 0870 770 4014

www.dentalhealth.org.uk

British Dental Association

See the BDA mouth at www.3dmouth.org

The Community Dietitian

**Abi Mogridge
Community Dietitian**

Community dietitians have two overriding aims. At a local and national level we work with other professionals to meet local and national health targets such as preventing and reducing the incidence of obesity, diabetes, heart disease and so forth. We also aim to meet the needs of individuals in our local area through providing services through community providers such as health centres, community hospitals and health promotion. Our work is both clinical, which is one-to-one work using therapeutic diets for people with medical conditions, and educational. Education is an important part of the clinical work, but dietitians also have an educational role, linked to the prevention of disease and promotion of health, with healthy groups of people and other professionals.

The day-to-day work of a dietitian tends to vary according to their specialist area. Specialist areas include paediatrics, enteral feeding, health promotion dietitian, diabetes and so forth. For example ,a dietitian who specialises in home enteral nutrition supports all patients who are being artificially fed. This includes anyone who cannot manage an oral diet or an adequate oral diet. They could be children or adults with cancers, learning disabilities, stroke or individuals with degenerative disease. They tend to visit the patient's home and plan their artificial nutrition according to their individual medical needs. Children would need very regular monitoring because their nutritional requirements will change as they grow. They will work closely with other health disciplines such as the district nurses, GPs and consultants.

The dietetic department is happy to receive referrals from anybody, including patients, as long as we can get accurate medical and up to date details. Most of our referrals come from GPs, consultants, practice nurses, district nurses and so forth. We do a number of clinics in different health centres and GP practices. The number of clinics can vary from one to eight clinics per month, according to need. Some might be seen only once, and others much longer. Our policy is to try not to see patients more than six times in a year. During a consultation we take a detailed diet, medical and social history and from this devise an appropriate diet plan. No patient is the same, and patients rarely have just one problem. We never send out dietary sheets in advance, we insist on seeing them first so that our dietary plan will meet their needs.

All our work, at the moment, is predominantly clinical. We would like to get more health promotion posts, so that we can work with Sure Start, schools, the inequalities teams and so forth, but we haven't got there yet. We can undertake individual sessions, talks and give support where we can. I contribute to the Healthy Eating Group, the steering group led by Kent Healthy Schools Healthy Eating coordinator, and have contributed to the training sessions that have been set up by the Breakfast Club coordinator for schools wanting to set up breakfast clubs. In other areas of the country health promotion dietitians are contributing to fruit schemes, breakfast clubs, staff and parent education and to the wider work of health promotion services. If a school would like the support of their local dietetics service, they need to approach their community dietetic service based at either their local primary care trust or acute hospital trust.

Useful Information

British Dietetic Association

Dietitians are registered with the Health Professions Council. Their professional body is the British Dietetic Association. The difference between a dietitian and a nutritionist is that dietitians can work with therapeutic diets, for people with medical conditions, and nutritionists cannot.

Dietitians in Obesity Management (UK) or DOM (UK) are a group of dietitians who work closely with the Association for the Study of Obesity and the National Obesity Forum. Its members include paediatric dietitians and community dietitians who specialise in the management of childhood obesity.

British Dietetic Association
5th Floor
Charles House
148/9 Great Charles Street
Queensway
Birmingham
B3 3HT

Tel. 0121 200 8080

www.bda.uk.com

The Nutrition Society

The Nutrition Society is the professional body that awards titles of Registered Nutritionist or Registered Public Health Nutritionist to appropriately qualified people who work as consultants in communities, in educational settings or abroad.

The Nutrition Society
10 Cambridge Court
210 Shepherds Bush Road
London
W6 7N7

www.nutritionsociety.org

Chapter Nine

Lesson Plans

The Whole-school Approach

It has been demonstrated that the most effective strategies to promote children's health in schools are those which are multifaceted, where the curriculum is supported by the school ethos and the local community (Lister-Sharp et al., 1999). Schools are strongly advised to integrate these lesson plans into a whole-school approach.

The Aim of the Lesson Plans

What we eat, our level of physical activity and our feelings about ourselves and our bodies are interdependent. We teach children about healthy food, healthy activity and healthy bodies and then wonder why we have escalating obesity, dieting and eating disorders. Perhaps this is because the reality is that children are dealing with a world which is promoting fast, fattening food, inactive leisure pursuits and unhealthy body images. In addition to social and environmental change and adult support, children need accurate information, the skills to make choices and a firm foundation of good self-esteem. These lesson plans aim to take children through a journey which enables them to learn about food, activity, their bodies and feelings in a holistic and meaningful way.

All the lessons are designed to develop children's communication and social skills, and many allow the children to explore feelings, including empathy with others, and to engage in problem-solving and joint decision making. In this way, the lessons make a contribution towards the social, emotional and behavioural skills identified by the National Healthy School Standard (DfES/DoH, 2004):

- being an effective and successful learner
- making and sustaining friendships
- dealing with and resolving conflict effectively and fairly
- being able to solve problems with others and alone
- managing strong feelings such as frustration, anger and anxiety
- recovering from setbacks and persisting in the face of difficulties
- working and playing cooperatively
- competing fairly and losing with dignity and respect for competitors
- recognising and standing up for one's rights and the rights of others
- understanding and valuing the differences between people and respecting the right of others to have beliefs and values different from one's own.

Inclusion of All Pupils and Differentiation

The lessons have been designed to try to meet the needs of all children, and they can be easily adapted to particular circumstances. Noreen Wetton (1986) advises that health education lessons should focus on enabling children to hear and understand the intended health message rather than focusing on the completion of tasks such as colouring or word searches. It is for this reason, and for reasons of inclusivity, that many of lessons are not heavily dependent upon reading and writing, although teachers can easily increase the demand on these skills by exchanging words for pictures or drawing if they think it appropriate. Most of the lessons are differentiated through outcome. Some are differentiated though peer assessment, and in others some might benefit from a writing frame. One lesson includes an upper Key Stage 2 activity and a lower Key Stage 2 activity. Most of the lessons can be adapted to individual, pair, group or whole class learning.

The Organisation of the Lessons

Teachers might use the lessons directly as written, whilst others will choose to modify them in order to better meet the needs of their pupils. The lessons are organised sequentially, but teachers can differentiate the sequence according to their pupils' needs. Examples of how five or six lessons could be grouped into half a term's planning are shown at the end of this chapter. Teachers should try to avoid teaching a lesson in isolation. Most of the lessons contain two or three main activities. Many also contain 'optional extra' activities which could be used as extension activities, or substituted for a main activity at the teacher's discretion. Most of the lessons include Fact Boxes so that teachers have key information at their fingertips. The 'optional extra' activities and Fact Boxes can provide pointers for setting homework.

Keeping Parents and Carers Informed

Chapter 8 has provided a number of examples showing how schools can involve and support parents and carers. In addition, it is advisable for teachers to write a letter to parents or carers explaining the purpose of these lessons and to discuss any anxieties, or indeed any good ideas, that they might have in advance. This might be particularly important for Lesson 3 and Lessons 12 to 19. Teachers could also consider how to involve parents and carers in homework tasks. Healthy Schools teams, at local health promotion departments, can support schools in their work with parents and carers.

An example letter to parents or carers:

Dear ....

This term, as part of our Personal, Social and Health Education teaching, Year 6 will be carrying out some work about the food which they eat, their bodies, their feelings and physical activity. The children will be asked to carry out activities such as making a note of what they eat and drink during a day and sharing this with the class. They will also be learning about why people come in all shapes and sizes, and how teasing and unkindness make us feel.

I welcome your involvement in this work, so please feel free to come and talk to me if you have any concerns or suggestions.

With best wishes,

....

The Lesson Plans

There are 19 lesson plans. Lesson 1 encourages the children to consider why they eat what they eat, before they are introduced to the principles of a healthy diet. Lessons 2 to 10 examine each food group and how they contribute to the Balance of Good Health. Having established what we should aim to eat, Lesson 11 addresses the timing of eating through the day. Lesson 12 prepares the children for Lessons 13 to 19 as these are potentially more sensitive in nature. Lessons 13 encourages the children to balance their food intake with activity. Lessons 14 and 15 provide information about changes in body shape and allow the children to explore their own and others' feelings. Lesson 18 examines the facts behind weight gain and weight loss. Lesson 19 brings the themes of food, activity, body image and feelings together.

Each lesson is prefaced by:

- Aim
- Objectives
- National Curriculum
- Duration
- Learning styles
- Skills
- Preparation and resources.

Within the lessons are ideas for:

- Assessment.

Each lesson ends with:

- Comments from educators.

Aims and objectives

The aim of the lesson is met through all activities, including the 'optional extra' activities. The objectives are measurable outcomes relating to the main activities only.

National Curriculum

Each lesson plan shows how the activities, including optional extra activities, meet the requirements for the National Curriculum at Key Stage 2.

Duration

The approximate duration of the lessons, consisting of the main activities only, are given. These will inevitably vary according to the needs and abilities of children.

Learning styles

Psychological research suggests that people process information in three ways, through what they see and look at (Visual), through what they hear and listen to (Auditory) and through their feelings and body activity (Kinaesthetic). We all use all three channels for our learning, but tend to have a preference for one. Visual learning includes looking at pictures or writing, auditory learning includes listening to a teacher or giving an oral presentation, and kinaesthetic learning includes role-plays or practical tasks (DfES, 2004b). In a classroom of children, their learning is likely to be maximised if lessons can allow learning using a variety of learning styles. For this reason, the relevant learning styles present within the main activities, excluding the optional extra activities, for each lesson are indicated.

Skills

Each lesson is labelled to show how the main activities develop children's skills.

Thinking skills include:

- Enquiry: asking relevant questions, posing and defining problems, planning how to research, predicting outcomes, anticipating responses, improving ideas.
- Problem-solving: identifying and understanding problems, planning solutions, monitoring progress, tackling a problem and reviewing a solution to a problem.
- Creative thinking: generating and extending ideas, suggesting hypotheses, applying imagination,

looking for alternative innovative outcomes.

- Information processing: locating and collecting relevant information, sorting, classifying, sequencing, comparing, contrasting, analysing part/whole relationships.

- Reasoning: giving reasons for opinions, drawing inferences, making deductions, using precise language to explain thinking, making judgements and decision on the basis of reasons or evidence.

- Evaluation: judging the value of what is read, heard or done, developing criteria for judging the value of work or ideas, having confidence in one's own judgements.

(DfES, 2004b)

Social, emotional and behavioural skills include:

- Self-awareness: understanding of self, knowing how one learns and relates to others, knowing what others are thinking and what they are feeling, use of self-awareness to organise and plan learning.

- Managing feelings: recognising and accepting feelings, managing anxiety, anger or demonstrating resilience in the face of difficulty.

- Motivation; enabling learners to take an active and enthusiastic part in learning, enabling learners to set goals and work towards them, to focus and concentrate, to persist when learning is difficult, to develop independence, resourcefulness and personal organisation.

- Empathy: understanding others, anticipating and predicting others' thoughts, feelings and perceptions, seeing things from another person's point of view and modifying one's own response if appropriate.

- Social skills: relating to others, taking an active part in a group, communicating with different audiences, resolving differences, supporting the learning of others.

(DfES, 2003)

These skills are identified in relation to the main activities of each lesson.

Preparation and resources

The preparatory tasks and resources required for the main activities are outlined at the beginning of each lesson.

Assessment

Ideas for assessment for learning are given within the lessons.

Comments from educators

Some of the activities have been carried out by teachers and school nurses, and their comments are given at the end of the lessons.

Detailed lesson plan

For teachers wishing to prepare a detailed lesson plan, an example is shown alongside Lesson 1.

Examples of weekly planning sheets

This chapter ends with two examples of Weekly Planning Sheets that provide examples of how lessons can be selected and combined as a five-week or six-week programme.

Lesson 1 Why Do We Eat What We Eat?

Aim: to highlight that people eat for a wide variety of reasons.

Objectives:

- to identify a wide range of reasons for children's own eating behaviour

- to produce a poster Why do we eat what we eat? for the display board.

National Curriculum: Sc2/2b; PSHE&Citz/4f

Duration: 60 minutes

Learning Styles: visual, auditory

Skills: creative thinking, reasoning, self-awareness, motivation, empathy, social skills

Preparation and resources:

- Each child might need a piece of paper and a pencil (optional).

- A large sheet of paper for display.

Activity

Ask the children, "Think about what you have eaten today," and, "What did you eat yesterday?" Working alone, in pairs or in groups, children could draw or write the foods they have eaten. Share some of the answers with the class.

"Why do we eat what we eat?" Encourage the children to brainstorm as many reasons they can think of, perhaps with some prompts such as, "Why did you eat sandwiches at lunch time? Why did you eat chocolate on Saturday? Why didn't you eat fish and chips for your breakfast?" Children could work in pairs or groups before feeding back to the class.

Write the reasons onto a large sheet of paper to display. Discuss the range of different reasons given and the underlying physical, psychological, social, cultural or spiritual influences on the children's eating.

Remind the children how babies are nurtured through feeding, and how it makes them feel content. Ask them, "How does eating make you feel?"

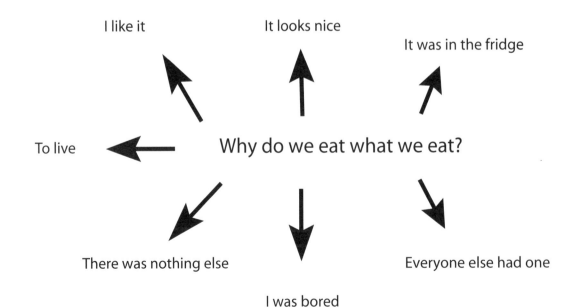

FACT BOX	
Why do we eat what we eat?	
hunger	appearance
health, allergy, medical	boredom
slimming	advertising
culture, religion	comfort
family lifestyle	habit
season, climate	cost
available in kitchen, shops, tuck shop	taste
able to be grown, transported, delivered	to be sociable
texture	friends like it
odour	ability to prepare or cook it
fashion	events, weddings, parties, cinema
someone else chooses for me	

Assessment

Cover up the reasons for eating. Ask each children to work in pairs and see how many of the reasons they can remember. Congratulate the pair that remembers the most.

Comments from educators

"A good mind mapping session resulting in some good evidence of understanding and some examples of the fact that certain foods do not travel across the social divide. I included making and decorating a folder. A good lesson." (Teacher Year 6)

Detailed Lesson Plan

For teachers wishing to prepare detailed lesson plans, Lesson 1 is presented to show how a teacher might wish to prepare for this lesson.

Introduction

Write the aim and objectives on the board. Ask the children, "Think about what you have eaten today." "What did you eat yesterday?" Write, "What do you eat?" on the board. Organise the children into pairs and ask them to draw or write as many items they can think of within three minutes. Share some of the answers with the class noting the range of foods.

Write, "Why do we eat what we eat?" on the board. Ask a child to explain why they think we have to eat. Build on this explanation and inform the pupils that we all have to eat to stay alive, but sometimes we choose to eat for other reasons. Ask them to think about why they chose to eat their breakfast or their lunch, and encourage them to think of a wide range of reasons from, "Because I was told to," to, "Everyone else was eating it," to, "I was bored."

Timing: 15 minutes

Main

Continuing to work in pairs, ask the children to discuss with their partner all their ideas about why they eat what they eat. Ask them to draw or write their ideas on a piece of paper. When they have exhausted their reasons, ask them to think about reasons why other children might eat what they eat. When they have finished ask them to discuss their lists with another pair of pupils. Explore some of the underlying physical, psychological, social, cultural or spiritual influences on children's eating.

Remind the class how babies are nurtured through feeding, and how it makes them feel content. Ask, "How does eating make you feel?"

Timing: 20-30 minutes

Plenary

Write, "Why do we eat what we eat?" on a large piece of paper. Ask each pair in turn to call out a reason, and write onto the paper, until all the reasons are given. Display on the notice board.

Timing: 10-15 minutes

Homework

Ask each child to ask their families or carers about why they eat what they eat, and bring their answers to school tomorrow.

Assessment

A specimen copy of work may be kept for a class or pupil portfolio.

Lesson 2 Introducing Food Groups

Aim: to introduce The Balance of Good Health food groups.

Objectives:

- to know that foods can be grouped into food groups

- to identify examples of which foods belong to which group, including those that belong to more than one group

- to produce a large Balance of Good Health plate for display.

National Curriculum: Sc2/2b; D&T/2a,2b,2d,5a; A&D/2b,2c,4b

Duration: 60 to 80 minutes

Learning Styles: visual, auditory, kinaesthetic

Skills: problem-solving, creative thinking, information processing, reasoning, motivation, social skills

Preparation and resources:

- Each child needs to bring two or three different types of clean packaging from food or drink, such as cans, boxes, wrappers, plastic containers for salad or vegetables and plastic bottles, into school. You might like to collect some additional examples in order to broaden the range.

- White board pens in colours: orange, green, pink/red, blue, yellow are optional.

- Large labels will be needed for each food group: a set for the display board, and a set for the assessment (Fruit and vegetables, Bread, other cereals and potatoes, Meat, fish and alternatives; Milk and dairy foods, Foods containing fat, Foods containing sugar).

- Prepare a giant (as large as possible) blank plate segmented to represent The Balance of Good Health plate for the display board. See the poster on the CD-ROM. Either cut up large pieces of coloured paper (orange, green, pink/red, blue, yellow) ready to be stuck onto the plate's segments or consider another method for quick colouring in.

- Prepare materials for children to draw, paint or make foods.

- Local Health Promotion Departments might be able to loan plastic foods and Balance of Good Health resources.

- An A3 copy of the worksheet Good Health showing a blank Balance of Good Health and small sized food wrappers for each pair of children is optional.

Activity 1

Ask the children to look at their packaging and distribute your examples to any child without. Ask the children to consider the shape, colour, pictures and what kind of food was inside packaging. How did the packaging keep the food fresh?

Introduce the idea that foods can be grouped in different ways. Write the food groups across the board, ideally using coloured pens as indicated.

Ask individual children to hold up their packaging. "What do you think was in it? Which group do you think it belongs to?" Begin to write lists of foods under the five headings.

Bread, other cereals and potatoes (orange)	Fruit and vegetables (green)	Meat, fish and alternatives (pink/red)	Milk and dairy foods (blue)	Foods containing fat. Foods containing sugar (yellow)
cornflakes	lettuce	fish fingers	milk	chocolate
bread	tomatoes	sausages	cheese	crisps

After each child's food or drink has been recorded, ask them to place their packages together next to the large label for the appropriate food group. Draw attention to any foods, perhaps by cutting the package into two, which belong in more than one group.

Ask the children to consider, "What other kinds of foods could be added to these groups? What kinds of food do not have any packaging?" Ask each child to draw, paint or make one of the missing items and add these to the groups of packaging.

Activity 2

Across a wall or display board, display a big, blank plate across a wall or notice board that shows only the segments.

Colour each segment, or stick appropriately coloured and shaped paper onto each segment. Around the outside, attach the large labels naming the food groups. Show the children how some segments are larger than others. Introduce the children to the idea that we ought to try to eat plenty of some foods in the larger segments and less of the foods in the smaller segments.

Staple or stick some of the packages onto the correct segments of the plate. Some food groups might have very many packages and are 'spilling over' whilst others might have much more space. "What could this mean?" "Do some belong to more than one group?"

Assessment

Label each corner of the room as a food group, and the centre as well. Read out a list of foods and drinks, some of which have not been discussed during the lesson, and ask the children to walk quietly, or point, to the food group area to which they think it belongs. Provide feedback.

Comments from educators

"Some good continuity from lesson one resulting in some understanding of food groups. I modified it to a personal level to enable understanding across the ability range." (Teacher Year 6)

Optional extra

Ask children to work in pairs, and give them a copy of the worksheet Good Health (page 156), possibly copied onto A3 paper. Ask them to label their Balance of Good Health sections. Give each pair a selection of food packages and ask them to place them on the correct section.

FACT BOX				
Bread, other cereals and potatoes	**Fruit and vegetables**	**Meat, fish and alternatives**	**Milk and dairy foods**	**Foods containing fat.** **Foods containing sugar**
high fibre breakfast cereals bread (white and wholemeal) pitta bread porridge other breakfast cereals pasta rice	apples peas cabbage, cauliflower, broccoli orange juice tomatoes tangerines, satsumas oranges carrots bananas sweetcorn onions, mushrooms and peppers salad vegetables (lettuce) canned fruit	minced beef poultry (chicken) baked beans eggs lamb chop white fish tuna kidney beans unsalted nuts	semi-skimmed milk cheeses yoghurt – low fat	crisps lemonade (non diet) fat spread (e.g. butter, margarine or low fat spread) and/or oil fondant cake

Lesson 3 What Are We Eating?

Aim: to begin to understand the importance of eating a variety of foods and a balance of foods for healthy eating.

Objectives:

- to reflect on children's own diets

- to be able to allocate children's own food and drink to the appropriate food groups

- to know that it is important to eat a variety of foods from different food groups.

National Curriculum: Sc2/2b; PSHE&Citz/3a; Ma2/4e; Ma4/1f2c

Duration: 60 minutes

Learning Styles: visual, auditory

Skills: problem-solving, information processing, reasoning, evaluation, self-awareness, social skills

Preparation and resources:

- An A4 booklet, *The Balance of Good Health* is available from the Food Standards agency (telephone 0845 6060667, e mail: foodstandards@ecologistics.co.uk) or through your local Health Promotion Department (optional).

- Each child needs a copy of the worksheet What I've Eaten Since Home Time Yesterday and a pencil.

- It is advisable to write a letter to parents and carers explaining the purpose of this work in advance, and to allay any anxieties that they might have.

- The day before, explain to the children, "Tomorrow we are going to look at what we are all eating again. When you go home after school I'd like you to write down everything that you eat and drink until you come back to school tomorrow."

Activity 1

The next morning, remind children about the five food groups by referring to The Balance of Good Health plate that was made in Lesson 2, or the booklet obtained from the Food Standards Agency.

Distribute the worksheet What I've Eaten Since Home Time Yesterday to pairs, or small groups, of children. Alternatively use paper plates made of white card.

Explain that the children are to draw or write the food that they ate since leaving school yesterday onto the blank plate. Explain how to record each food item into the correct food group.

Activity 2

After lunch help the children to add their mid-morning snacks and their lunch to the blank plate.

Draw a blank plate on the board. Ask the children to call out examples of foods in each food group, and write these on the board. Children could be asked to add these to their plates. Point out how much variety is represented. Ask, "Which food group contains the most foods?" "Which food group contains the fewest foods?" "What does this plate tell us about what we are eating?" Consider 'more of and less of' and 'better alternatives', avoiding labels such as 'bad' or 'good', or 'healthy' or 'unhealthy'. Explain that eating a variety of foods across the plate is good for health.

Assessment

Observe the children's work and ask questions to check understanding.

Comments from educators

"Some excellent work here that I am going to use as classroom display. The children drew two plates on one sheet of plain A4 paper. On plate 1, they drew and labelled a typical evening meal in their household, and on plate 2 they drew what they understand to be a healthy meal. The difference was, in some cases, amazing." (Teacher Year 6)

Optional extra

Ask the children to discuss why they ate the food, in pairs or as a class. These could be written onto their plates. Refer to the poster Why do we eat what we eat? produced in Lesson 1, and add any new reasons.

Optional extra

The data from the children's balanced plates could be used to provide a summary of the children's balance of eating as a class. Working in groups, children could enter their findings onto a database in order to produce graphs showing the foods eaten in the group and the number of children who ate them.

What I've Eaten Since Home Time Yesterday

Lesson 4 Fruit And Vegetables

Aim: to encourage children to want to explore and eat fruit and vegetables.

Objectives:

- to extend children's awareness of a range of fruit and vegetables
- to enhance children's sensory perceptions of fruit and vegetables
- to identify a portion of fruit or vegetables
- to know that five portions of fruit and vegetables are recommended per day.

National Curriculum: Sc2/2b; PSHE&Citz/2k,3a; Language; En1/1b,1e,1f,2a,8a,8b,8c,9c; En3/9c;Mu/1c,4b

Duration: 90 minutes

Learning Styles: visual, auditory, kinaesthetic

Skills: problem-solving, creative thinking, information processing, evaluation, self-awareness, motivation, social skills

Preparation and resources:

- Each child needs a piece of paper and a pencil.
- A small selection of fruit and vegetables presented in single portions.
- Each group of children will need a copy of the worksheet What is a Portion of Fruit and Vegetables?
- Some washed and prepared fruit or vegetables for eating are optional.

Activity 1

Remind the class about The Balance of Good Health plate that was made in Lesson 2, or the booklet obtained from the Food Standards Agency, and refer them to the Fruit and Vegetables group.

Write a series of letters on the board. These could be random, the name of the school, the name of the day or month, or a sporting celebrity.

P T O R A C L B

Ask the children to work in pairs. They have five or ten minutes to think about all the fruit and vegetables that begin with one of the letters. They could be given access to a dictionary.

After five or ten minutes write all the fruit and vegetables on the board. "Can we think of any more? Which of these have you tasted? What do they taste like?"

potato	tomato	orange	rhubarb	apple
cauliflower	lemon	broccoli	corn	tangerine
cabbage	lime	banana	lettuce	

Activity 2

Explain that we should try to eat five portions of fruit and vegetables each day. Write '5' next to the fruit and vegetables section of the Balance of Good Health plate. Show the class some examples of fruit and vegetable portions. Write on the board some examples of portions.

Ask the children to work in groups. Give each group the worksheet What is a Portion of Fruit and Vegetables? showing a selection of fruits and vegetables. Each group need to decide how much, or how many of each fruit or vegetable, comprise a portion.

Taking one fruit or vegetable at a time, ask the groups to feed back their answers. Draw or write on the board, or demonstrate using the real items if they are available.

Activity 3

Ask the children to work in small groups. Each group is given a fruit or vegetable and asked to write down four good things about it. Prompt with questions if necessary. "Is it juicy/ crispy/ colourful?"

Explain that each group is going to make up a jingle to sell their product to others. Firstly, the class will make up one together. The teacher chooses a fruit or vegetable and the class helps to identify four good features. These are written on the board.

apple – crispy, fresh, sweet, juicy

Four children are asked to stand.

One child says, "Apple".

The next child says, "Crispy".

The next child says, "Apple".

The next child says, "Fresh," and so forth.

This can be developed to a simple rap or rhythm,

"Apple, crispy, apple, fresh, apple, sweet, apple, juicy."

It could be developed into a poem or jingle.

"Apple crunchy, apple sweet

Apple on my plate to eat

Apple juicy, apple crisp

Always on the shopping list."

Each group of children are asked to develop their own raps, jingles or poems using the words associated with their own fruit or vegetable.

Some of the groups might like to perform for the class. The children could be asked to evaluate the performances, "Were you convinced that the fruit or vegetable sounds good to eat?" "Were the words clear to hear?" "Was it catchy?"

Assessment

Ask each group of children to name two positive qualities of a fruit or a vegetable that they might not have thought about before this lesson.

Comment from educators

"Children were asked to link names of fruit and vegetables with letters in their own name. They were able to produce a very large class list of fruit and vegetables. Then the lesson was modified and the children compiled a list of fruit and vegetables that they liked and didn't like. This was followed by a discussion about the reasons for this. Next the children worked in groups and chose their own fruit or vegetable. They wrote four words to describe the good things about it and then wrote a rap, poem or jingle. The children were hardworking throughout and enjoyed the activity. We discussed how this kind of activity could be developed and decided that the possibilities were endless. It could be linked to Music by applying composing skills for the rap or jingle. In Art, the use of artists' work could be explored where fruit and vegetables are the main focus of the work, such as Archimoldo's use of fruit and vegetables to create faces. Some children who have challenging behaviour were completely 'on task' and produced excellent work."

Optional extra

Ask for a volunteer. Blindfold the child and give them a fruit or vegetable to hold. Ask the child to describe the texture and odour. If appropriate, would the child be willing to eat a little? Can they describe it? Can they guess what it is? Would anyone else like to taste some? Encourage all the children to taste some samples.

Repeat for further fruits and vegetables.

Optional extra

Ask the children to work in groups. "What influences how you feel about food?" For example, encourage the children to think about TV, posters, what friends and family eat or say, the packaging, special occasions and so forth. Can the children identify why they may have positive or negative perceptions about a fruit or a vegetable?

FACT BOX
We should eat at least 5 portions of fruit and vegetables a day. **What is a portion?**

For large fruit: half a grapefruit or one slice of papaya or one large slice of pineapple

For medium fruit: one apple, banana, pear, orange, nectarine or a sharon fruit.

For small fruits: two or more plums, satsumas, kiwi fruit, apricots.

For very small fruit it depends: seven strawberries, 14 cherries, 6 lychees.

For dried fruit: one tablespoon of, for example, raisins, currants, sultanas.

For tInned fruit: roughly the same quantity as that you'd eat of a fresh fruit, for example, two pear halves

For juice: one medium (150 ml) glass of 100% fruit juice which only counts as one portion no matter how much you drink

For green vegetables: two broccoli spears, 8 cauliflower florets, four heaped tablespoons of kale, spring greens or green beans

For cooked vegetables: three heaped tablespoons of cooked vegetables such as carrots, peas or sweetcorn

For salad vegetables: three sticks of celery, two inch piece of cucumber, one medium tomato, seven cherry tomatoes, one cereal bowl of mixed salad

For tinned and frozen vegetables: roughly the same as you would eat for a fresh portion.

What is a Portion of Fruit and Vegetables?

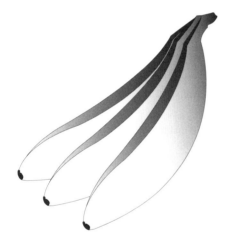

Lesson 5 Bread, Other Cereals and Potatoes

Aim: to encourage children to understand the benefits of eating plenty of bread, cereals and potatoes.

Objectives:

- to raise awareness about some of the foods in the bread, cereals and potatoes food group

- to identify some higher fibre foods through observation

- to identify a portion of bread, other cereals or potatoes.

National Curriculum: Sc2/2b; Sc3/1a,3a; PSHE&Citz/3a.

Duration: 80 minutes

Learning Styles: visual, auditory, kinaesthetic

Skills: enquiry, information processing, reasoning, self-awareness, social skills.

Preparation and resources:

- You will need a selection of foods from this food group, perhaps concentrating on the foods that may be new to the children.

- You will need a selection of whole grains such as oat groats, pot barley or wheat that can be obtained from health foods shops, along with teaspoons and paper towels.

- You will need six bowls of different breakfast cereals.

- Each group of children will need a slice of white bread and a slice of granary bread.

- You could display pictures showing whole grains and plants so that children can see where cereals come from.

- You might need a cup of white flour, cup of granary flour, large bowl and a sieve (optional).

- Each child needs a piece of paper and a pencil. A prepared grid is optional.

- A pestle and mortar, or electric coffee grinder, per group of children is optional.

Activity 1

Remind the class about The Balance of Good Health plate that was made in Lesson 2 or the booklet obtained from the Food Standards Agency. Refer them to the bread, other cereals and potatoes group. Find out how many foods they can remember go into this group.

Explain how we need to eat plenty of these foods every day because they fill us up and give us energy. About a third of our food intake needs to come from this group that means eating at least one food from this group at each meal. Write 'eat more' next to the appropriate section on the Balance of Good Health plate.

Distribute examples of foods from this group. Working in pairs or groups, encourage the children to discuss the texture, colour, and where appropriate, the odour. Pass the foods around the class.

Activity 2

Ask if anyone has eaten any bread today. We eat bread in many ways. It comes in many shapes and sizes. Ask the children to work in groups and to think of as many kinds of bread that they can. Feed back to the class.

Give each group a piece of white and granary bread, and ask them to look at the bread carefully. Can they identify how the two breads are similar and how they are different. Each group should consider the colour, texture and odour. The children could be invited to taste a small piece of the bread (check for any wheat/gluten allergies). Feed back to the class.

"Who knows which piece of bread contains the most fibre? How can you tell?"

Explain that many high fibre foods, but not all, are brown and textured. Some are very fibrous and some contain whole grains of wheat or rye that we can see and taste.

Activity 3

Provide the children with some whole grains that they can crush with a teaspoon onto a paper towel. Explain that whole grains are ground to make flour, an important ingredient of bread. Explain that wholemeal/wholegrain/high fibre foods like bread contain all of the grain, and sometimes wholegrains. Nothing has been taken away.

Refer the children to pictures of whole grains and plants.

Continue to work in groups and ask the children if they can add to their previous answers about why the two breads are different. Share answers with the class.

Explain how lower fibre foods, such as white bread, do not contain all of the grain, nor do they contain the whole grains, because some of the grain has been sieved out.

Optional extra

Show the children the cup of white flour and sieve into large bowl. Note how nothing is left in the sieve. Pour the granary flour through a sieve to separate whole grains from flour. Explain that the whole grains are particularly rich in fibre, as well as goodies such as vitamins. Children might like to taste the whole grains.

Activity 4

Display six bowls each containing different types of breakfast cereals. Ask the children how they might identify which is higher in fibre. What criteria could they use? Write the names of the cereals next to the bowls.

> **Cheerios**
>
> **Ready Brek**
>
> **Rice Krispies**
>
> **Shreddies**
>
> **Sugar Puffs**
>
> **Weetabix.**

Ask the children to work in pairs, and identify which cereals contain the most and least fibre by looking carefully at the colour and texture. Ask them to record their answers in a list, with the most at the top and the least at the bottom.

Discuss the children's answers, asking why they came to their conclusions, and provide the correct answers using the information given in the Fact Box. Note that some higher fibre cereals are easier to identify by observation than others.

Assessment

Mix up the breakfast cereals, and ask the children to advise the teacher how to put them in rank order of higher fibre and lower fibre.

Comments from educators

The children could not think of a very wide range of bread types. Some responses were, 'Thick sliced,' or, 'Hovis,' so this needed explanation. Children were amazed that some cereals had the same amount of fibre as a slice of bread, even though the amount of cereal was large (100 g). We also researched the Recommended Daily Amount of fibre and again the children were amazed at how much it was. This led us to think about where fibre is found in our daily diet and the children are going to search for fibre content on packets."

Optional extra

Place different bowls of cereals on separate tables. Ask the children to record details about the colour, texture and smell of the cereals onto a grid. Groups of children could be asked to start at one table, and move clockwise when you ask them to move on.

Optional extra

Each group of children could be given a pestle and mortar, or an electric coffee grinder, in order to grind whole grains of wheat or barley to make their own flour.

FACT BOX			
Bread and cereals			
	Fibre (NSP) per 100 grams*	**Portion**	**Fibre (NSP) per portion**
White bread	1.9 g	1 slice, 30 g	3.7 g
Granary bread	3.3 g	1 slice, 30 g	3.9 g
White, plain flour	3.1 g	1 slice, 30 g	0.9 g
Wholemeal flour	9.0 g	1 slice, 30 g	2.7 g
White rice, easy cook, raw	0.4 g	2 rounded tbsp	0.2 g
Brown rice (raw)	1.9 g	2 rounded tbsp	0.9 g
Spaghetti, white, raw	2.9 g	100 g	2.9 g
Spaghetti, wholemeal, raw	8.4 g	100 g	8.4 g
Oatmeal, quick cook, raw	7.1 g	2 rounded tbsp	3.5 g
Food Standards Agency (2002) *McCance and Widdowson's The Composition of Foods.* 6th summary edn., Cambridge: Royal Society of Chemistry			

FACT BOX			
Breakfast Cereals			
	Fibre (NSP) per 100 grams*	**Portion normally eaten**	**Fibre (NSP) per portion**
All Bran	24.5 g	1 rounded tbsp (15 g)	3.7 g
Bran Flakes	13 g	2 rounded tbsp (30 g)	3.9 g
Cheerios	6.2 g	2 rounded tbsp (30 g)	1.8 g
Coco Pops	0.6 g	2 rounded tbsp (30 g)	0.2 g
Cornflakes	0.9 g	2 rounded tbsp (30 g)	0.3 g
Crunchy Nut Cornflakes	0.8 g	2 rounded tbsp (30 g)	0.2 g
Frosties	0.6 g	2 rounded tbsp (30 g)	0.2g
Fruit 'n Fibre	7 g	2 rounded tbsp (30 g)	2.1g
Muesli	6.4 g	1 rounded tbsp (15 g)	0.9 g
Oat Bran Flakes with raisins	10 g	2 rounded tbsp (30 g)	3 g
Oatso Simple (porridge)	9 g	2 rounded tbsp (30 g)	2.4 g
Puffed Wheat	5.6 g	2 rounded tbsp (30 g)	1.7 g
Ready Brek	8.0 g	2 rounded tbsp (30 g)	2.4 g
Rice Krispies	0.7 g	2 rounded tbsp (30 g)	0.2 g
Ricicles	0.4 g	2 rounded tbsp (30 g)	0.1 g
Shredded Wheat	9.8 g	1 shredded wheat (20 g)	1.9 g
Shreddies	9.5 g	2 rounded tbsp (30 g)	2.8 g
Special K	2 g	2 rounded tbsp (30 g)	0.6 g
Sugar Puffs	3.2 g	2 rounded tbsp (30 g)	0.9 g
Sultana Bran	10 g	2 rounded tbsp (30 g)	3 g
Weetabix	9.7 g	2 weetabix (40 g)	3.8 g
Food Standards Agency (2002) *McCance and Widdowson's The Composition of Foods*, 6th summary edn., Cambridge: Royal Society of Chemistry			

Lesson 6 Milk And Dairy Foods

Aim: to raise awareness of the nutritional value of milk.

Objectives:

- to know some of the health benefits of milk

- to identify how skimmed, semi-skimmed and whole milk differ.

National Curriculum: Sc2/2a,2b,2e; PSHE&Citz/3a, Ma2/1f; Ma3/4a; Language; En1/1b

Duration: 60 to 80 minutes

Learning Styles: visual, auditory, kinaesthetic

Skills: problem-solving, information processing, reasoning, motivation, social skills

Preparation and resources:

- Collect three empty plastic milk bottles. These should have contained whole, semi-skimmed and skimmed milk. Cover the large words: WHOLE, SEMI-SKIMMED or SKIMMED on the labels with a removable label. On the back of each carton write a large figure showing the fat content, and the calcium content as shown in the Fact Box. Cover each of these with a removable label. Leave the blue, green and red coloured tops on each bottle.

- Three jugs labelled 1, 2 and 3 filled with the three types of milk. You need to record which jug contains which type of milk.

- Three cups per group of children.

- Three teaspoons per child.

- Paper towels in case of spillage.

- Prepare a grid if you wish groups to record their answers (optional).

- You might wish to provide a selection of alternative drinks (optional).

Activity 1

Remind the class about the Balance of Good Health plate made in Lesson 2 or the booklet obtained from the Food Standards Agency. Refer them to the milk and dairy foods group. "Which foods are grouped as milk and dairy foods?" Explain that we need to eat moderate amounts, two to three servings, each day, and write 'moderate' next to the appropriate section on the plate. Show the class examples of servings. "How many servings of cheese do you think are on a whole pizza?" Draw the size of the pizza on the board.

FACT BOX

We should eat 2 to 3 servings of milk and dairy foods a day.

What is a serving?

1/3 pint (200 ml) milk

small pot yoghurt (6 oz, 150 g)

matchbox size piece of cheese (1.2 oz, 30 g)

Try to choose lower fat versions such as semi-skimmed milk, low fat yoghurts and reduced fat cheese.

Activity 2

Ask the children, "Who drinks milk? Is it only humans?" Refer to the importance of suckling for all animals, and to the importance of breast milk for babies.

We drink milk in many ways, how many ways can you think of?" Milk is in drinks, sauces, ice cream, custard etc. Do the children know where milk comes from?

Ask the children, in pairs or groups to draw or write what milk contains. Ask a member of the group to draw or write one suggestion on the board. Ask the class to raise their hands if they agree with the suggestion. Put a tally of those that agree next to the suggestion. Repeat, and after a few suggestions tick the correct ones and reveal that milk is made up of:

- water (very important to keep all our body healthy)
- protein (to help us to grow)
- fat (for energy and warmth)
- milk sugar (for energy, and which is different to ordinary sugar, and doesn't harm our teeth)
- vitamins and minerals (goodies which help to keep us healthy)
- calcium (for growing and maintaining strong bones and teeth).

Do the children know how each nutrient benefits the body?

Activity 3

Organise the children into groups, and provide each group with three empty cups, labelled 1, 2 and 3 along with three teaspoons for each child. Show them the three empty milk bottles with their red, green and blue tops. "Do you know why milk has different coloured tops?" Explain that the colours relates to skimmed, semi-skimmed or whole milk, but try to avoid explaining what these definitions mean.

Pour jug 1 milk into cups labelled 1. Repeat for jugs 2 and 3 accordingly. Explain that each group is going to analyse the milk. Each group should discuss, draw, write or record onto a grid:

- colour (white, cream, yellow)
- appearance (streaky, watery)
- odour (strong, weak)
- taste (creamy, watery, tasty)

Remind children of the importance of using a clean teaspoon for each taste. Check for lactose intolerance.

Can the children guess the identity of the milk? Collate each group's findings onto a grid on the board.

Remove the labels covering the words WHOLE, SEMI-SKIMMED and SKIMMED and explain how these relate to the amount of fat in the milk.

WHOLE – the milk from the cow

SEMI-SKIMMED – the visible cream which we can see at the top of whole milk has been removed

SKIMMED – the milk is specially treated to remove extra fat

Reveal the figures showing the fat content on each bottle. Explain how we tend to eat higher fat foods too often and should try to eat them less frequently. "Which milk do you think is the best for someone who wants to try and eat less fat?"

Explain how babies drink bottle milk or breast milk. Children under two should have whole milk. Between two and five most children can have either whole or semi-skimmed milk. After five years old, most children can drink any of the three types, though many nutritionists would recommend semi-skimmed.

Reveal the type of milk in each sample and encourage the children to reflect on their reasons for their answers.

Activity 4

Ask the children if they can remember what else we said was in milk, besides fat. Explain that one of the really special things about milk is that it is one of the best sources of calcium. Write the word 'calcium' on the board.

"Do you think that each bottle of milk contains the same amount of calcium or different amounts?"

Reveal the figures on the back of the bottles to show that, although the fat content can be very different, the calcium content stays almost the same.

FACT BOX			
	Pint of skimmed milk (568 mls)	**Pint of semi-skimmed milk (568 mls)**	**Pint of whole milk (568 mls)**
Protein	19.4 g	19.4 g	19 g
Calcium	0.7 g (704 mg)	0.7 g (693 mg)	0.7 g (676 mg)
Fat	0.6 g	9.4 g	23 g
Milk also provides a good range of vitamins and minerals			
Milk is a major provider of calcium			
Calcium in milk is readily absorbed by the body			
Calcium gives bones their strength			
Calcium is particularly important when bones are growing			
Bones grow rapidly throughout childhood			
Milk is kind to teeth because milk sugar does not damage teeth and calcium helps to repair teeth			

Assessment

Ask the children to recall as many reasons as they can for why we should drink milk. Organise children into groups, and tell them that they have been employed by the Dairy Council to invent an advertising slogan to promote milk. Give examples of slogans, for example, 'An apple a day keeps the doctor away' and 'Go to work on an egg'. Choosing one reason for drinking milk, ask each group to present their slogans to the class.

Comments from educators

"Children enjoyed the topic of milk and were interested in the difference between the three types. Lots of misconceptions about how healthy each type was. The lesson contained lots of discussion. I ended the lesson by asking pupils to design a poster to encourage other children to drink milk."

Optional extra

You could show the calcium content of alternative drinks and use the data to discuss units of measurement.

FACT BOX		
		Calcium
Cola	can/bottle (330 mls)	19.8 mg
Diet cola	can/bottle (330 mls)	19.8 mg
Lemonade	can/bottle (330 mls)	16.5 mg
Sunny Delight	can/bottle (330 mls)	3.3 mg
Fruit squash (diluted)	glass (200 mls)	1.5 mg
Orange juice (unsweetened)	carton (300 mls)	30 mg
Skimmed milk	bottle/carton (568 mls)	704 mg
Semi-skimmed milk	bottle/carton (568 mls)	693 mg
Whole milk	bottle/carton (568 mls)	676 mg

Lesson 7 Meat, Fish and Alternatives

Aim: to introduce children to the importance of meat, fish and alternatives.

Objectives:

- to know some key reasons why eating some meat, fish and alternatives is good for health

- to be aware of two ways in which people's choices of foods can differ according to their beliefs.

National Curriculum: Sc2/2b; En1/2a,2c; PSHE&Citz/2e,2i,3a,4b,4f

Duration: 60 minutes

Learning Styles: auditory, visual, kinaesthetic

Skills: problem-solving, information processing, reasoning, motivation, empathy, social skills

Preparation and resources:

- You, and/or the children, will need the worksheet Sunita Wins the Race.

- Each child needs a piece of paper and pencils or crayons.

Activity 1

Remind the class about The Balance of Good Health plate made in Lesson 2 or the booklet obtained from the Food Standards Agency. Refer them to the meat, fish and alternatives group, and tell them that we need to eat moderate amounts from this group each day. Write 'moderate' next to the appropriate section on the plate. We should try to choose lower fat versions where we can. Some meat products such as beef burgers and sausages can be high in fat. We should eat two servings of fish each week, one of which should be an oily fish such as mackerel, sardines or tuna.

Explain that you are going to read them a story that shows why the foods in this food group are important. After this you are going to re-read the story and ask the children to draw and write about these foods.

Alternatively, ask the pupils to work in mixed ability groups, and ask the better readers to read the story instead of yourself, as outlined below. Each group can record their answers together.

Read the whole story Sunita Wins the Race to the class.

Sunita Wins the Race

In 2003 children at Raynes Park School cracked the world record for the largest egg and spoon race in the world. 859 children ran the race, and over 700 eggs were carried safely across the finishing line. In first place was Sunita from Year 6, and Mike Pen from the local newspaper ran up to interview her.

"Why eggs?" he asked.

"Eggs are a great fast food because they contain protein which helps us to grow and grow," puffed Sunita.

"What other foods help us to grow?" asked Mike.

Sunita sat down on the grass to catch her breath. "Well all meat contains protein. So it is good to eat chicken, beef, liver, mince, burgers and turkey. My Mum says that the best meat is the kind which is less fatty, because too much fat is not good for you." Sunita said, "Some people eat ham, bacon and sausages, but I don't because I am a Muslim. Some people don't eat other meats, such as beef, because of their religion too. My friend Milly doesn't eat meat at all because she's vegetarian."

"What's a vegetarian?" asked Mike.

"It's someone who chooses not to eat meat or fish."

"So how do they get the protein that they need to grow?"

"Vegetarians eat other foods which contain protein instead, such as eggs, nuts and beans."

"Is that healthy?" asked Mike as he scribbled on his note pad.

"Yes, if you make sure that you eat a wide variety of foods. Milly eats lots of foods. She tells me that beans on toast with a glass of fruit juice is a really good healthy meal for vegetarians."

"So what are you going to have for your lunch now?" Mike asked as Sunita got up to go. "Fish fingers," she replied. "Fish is a very good growing food too!"

Mike needed to hurry back to the office to write the article about the egg and spoon race. He checked his notes. "So protein is needed to grow, and it is in eggs, chicken, beef, liver, mince, burgers, turkey, ham, bacon, sausages, and fish."

"Is there anything else I need to know?" he asked as Sunita got up to go. "They all contain goodies such as iron, zinc and vitamins which means they keep our bodies healthy. We couldn't have beaten the world record without them!"

Re-read the first section of the story

Sunita Wins the Race

In 2003 children at Raynes Park School cracked the world record for the largest egg and spoon race in the world. 859 children ran the race, and over 700 eggs were carried safely across the finishing line. In first place was Sunita from Year 6, and Mike Pen from the local newspaper ran up to interview her.

"Why eggs?" he asked.

"Eggs are a great fast food because they contain protein which helps us to grow and grow," puffed Sunita.

"What other foods help us to grow?" asked Mike.

Sunita sat down on the grass to catch her breath. "Well all meat contains protein. So it is good to eat chicken, beef, liver, mince, burgers and turkey. My Mum says that the best meat is the kind which is less fatty, because too much fat is not good for you."

"Protein helps us to grow. Can you draw and label all the foods which contain lots of protein?" Read the section again, slowly, giving the children time to draw and label their foods.

Discuss the children's drawings, "Why did you draw that?" and then continue the story.

Sunita said, "Some people eat ham, bacon and sausages, but I don't because I am a Muslim. Some people don't eat other meats, such as beef, because of their religion too."

Ask the children to draw ham, bacon and sausages because these are good sources of protein too. Explain that there is some meat that are not eaten by some people because of their religious beliefs. Does this apply to some of the children in the class?

"Sunita cannot eat ham, bacon and sausages. Looking at your drawings, can you tell me which foods can she eat instead?"

Continue reading the story.

Sunita continued, "My friend Milly doesn't eat meat at all because she's vegetarian."

"What's a vegetarian?" asked Mike.

"It's someone who chooses not to eat meat or fish."

"So how do they get the protein that they need to grow?"

"Vegetarians eat other foods which contain protein instead, such as eggs, nuts and beans."

"Is that healthy?" asked Mike as he scribbled on his note pad.

"Yes, if you make sure that you eat a wide variety of foods. Milly eats lots of foods. She tells me that beans on toast with a glass of fruit juice is a really good healthy meal for vegetarians."

"What do vegetarians choose not to eat? What can they eat instead? Add these foods to your drawings" (see Fact Box). Read the section of the story again, slowly, giving the children time to draw. Discuss their drawings, and any issues that might arise about vegetarianism.

Continue the story.

"So what are you going to have for your lunch now?" Mike asked as Sunita got up to go. "Fish fingers," she replied. "Fish is a very good growing food too!"

"So what other food can we add to our drawings?"

Continue with the story.

Mike needed to hurry back to the office to write the article about the egg and spoon race. He checked his notes. "So protein is needed to grow, and it is in …"

Ask the children to call out all the foods in their drawings.

"Is there anything else I need to know?" he asked as Sunita got up to go. "They all contain goodies such as iron, zinc and vitamins which means they keep our bodies healthy. We couldn't have beaten the world record without them!"

Activity 2

Working in groups, pupils could be given three pieces of paper, one for a vegetarian, one for a Muslim and one for someone who eats healthily. Ask them to write or draw three foods from the meat, fish and alternatives group that would be suitable for each person, for one day. Their answers could be marked by other groups.

Assessment

Write 'True or false?' on the board. Either working individually, in pairs, groups or in two teams ask the children to stand up if they think the statement is true, and to remain sitting if they think the statement is false. Read out each statement.

True or false?

Eggs are a great food because they contain protein. (T)

Protein stops you from growing. (F)

Chicken contains protein and helps you to grow. (T)

Muslims do not eat ham and bacon. (T)

Vegetarians don't eat meat. (T)

Vegetarians need to eat a wide variety of food. (T)

Nuts do not contain protein. (F)

Beans contain protein. (T)

We should try to eat lots of fish because it is good for us. (T)

FACT BOX

In order to be useful to our bodies, we need to eat 'complete' proteins.

Animal sources of protein such as eggs, meat and fish contain 'complete' proteins.

Vegetables sources of protein such as bread and beans contain 'incomplete' proteins.

However, if they are eaten together at the same meal they join to form 'complete' proteins.

Fruit juice is not a good source of protein. However, it is particularly good to drink fruit juice with meals because the vitamin C helps the iron from meat and other foods to be absorbed into our bodies.

FACT BOX						
	Indian Punjab		Gujarat		Pakistan	Bangladesh
	Sikhs	Hindus	Hindus	Muslims	Muslims	Muslims
Meat and fish	no beef	no beef	no beef	no pork	no pork	no pork
	Some vegetarians others eat mainly chicken or mutton	Mostly vegetarians	Mostly vegetarians	Halal meat only (usually chicken or mutton)	Halal meat only (usually chicken or mutton)	Halal meat only (usually chicken or mutton)
	No fish	No fish	Some fish	Little if any fish	Little fish	A lot of fresh and dried fish
Eggs	Not a major part of the diet	Not eaten by strict vegetarians	Not eaten by strict vegetarians	Usually hard-boiled, fried or omelette	Usually hard-boiled, fried or omelette	Usually hard-boiled, fried or omelette (in curries)
Pulses e.g. beans, peas, lentils	Major sources of protein	Major sources of protein	Major sources of protein	Important	Important	Important
Health Education Authority (1991) *Nutrition in Minority Ethnic Groups: Asians and Afro-Caribbeans in the United Kingdom*. London: HEA						
Orthodox Jews eat no pork, no 'flightless birds', no shellfish or fish without fins, and do not eat meat and dairy foods together.						

Comments from educators

"Good story to introduce protein. Pupils enjoyed the topic and were able to relate to previous work. Pace was fast. We finished by adding additional foods to the children's drawings." (Teacher Year 3)

Optional extra

Using your knowledge about the medical profile of the class, you could extend this lesson to explore medical conditions that require modified or restricted diets. The school nurse, community dietitian and/or school caterers could provide guidance.

Lesson 8 Foods Containing Sugar

Aim: to raise awareness of sugar in foods.

Objectives:

- to know that too much sugar is unhealthy

- to identify some examples of high and low sugar foods and drinks

- to explore some of the ways to find out what is in our food and drink

- to practise social skills in relation to food and drink.

National Curriculum: Sc2/2a,2b; PSHE&Citz/3a,4a,4b,5g; En1/4b,11a,11b,11c; Ma4/1d,1e,1f

Duration: 80 minutes

Learning Styles: visual, auditory, kinaesthetic.

Skills: enquiry, problem-solving, creative thinking, information processing, reasoning, evaluation, self awareness, managing feelings, motivation, empathy, social skills.

Preparation and resources:

- You will need a selection of food and drink containers/packaging. These may or may not contain the contents. Some of these could be pictures instead.

- You will need a packet of sugar, a teaspoon and several small plates.

Activity 1

Remind the class about the Balance of Good Health plate made in Lesson 2 or the booklet obtained from the Food Standards Agency and refer them to the Foods containing Sugar group.

Explain that today they are going to think about the foods that contain a lot of sugar.

"What kinds of foods contain a lot of sugar? Can you think of any drinks which contain lots of sugar?" Ask the children to work in pairs and draw or write as many items they can think of in two minutes. Ask the children to feed back their answers.

"How do foods and drinks which are high in sugar affect our health?" Write suggestions on the board. Discuss the damaging effects of sugar on the teeth, how sugar does not contain any goodies like vitamins and minerals, and by eating too much sugary food we won't have enough room to eat foods which are going to help us to grow and feel healthy.

Show the class a rounded teaspoon of sugar. "Can you guess how many teaspoons of sugar children can have in one day, before they are eating too much?" Count out ten teaspoons of sugar onto the plate. Emphasise that the maximum of ten teaspoons includes both sugar that we can see and sugar that is hidden in our food. Do the children think they eat more or less than this? Emphasise that we should all be trying to moderate our sugar consumption. Avoid the misunderstanding that less than ten teaspoons is being endorsed.

Hold up an item of food or drink. "What do you think is inside this? How can we find out what is inside our food?" Explore how the food looks and tastes and the different examples of food and drink packaging. Consider the pictures, colours and words. "Sometimes we can't see what is in our food. It is hidden." Draw the children's attention to the list of ingredients and explain that they are shown in order of weight. Explain that by reading the label people can see whether there is sugar in foods and drinks.

"How many teaspoons of sugar do you think are in this?" Spoon out the correct teaspoons of sugar onto a plate and place this next to the item. Ask the children to consider whether they would have known that there was sugar in this food by just looking at the pictures on the packaging.

Repeat with other foods and drinks. Discuss how easy it is to reach ten teaspoons of sugar.

Arrange the foods and drinks into rank order showing highest sugar to lowest sugar content.

Ask the children, as a class or in groups, to think of lower sugar alternatives to a variety of foods and drinks. "Think about how sweet they are to taste." "Which drink has less sugar than this fizzy pop?" "What snack has less sugar than this bar of chocolate?" Write some examples on the board.

Finish the activity by emphasising it is the frequency of sugar consumption that most people need to reduce.

Optional extra

Give each group of children three or four food or drink containers/packages, or pictures of food and drink. Ask them to try and guess which might have the highest and lowest sugar content and put them in rank order. "Think carefully about what the food looks like and tastes like." "Why did you rank the foods in this way?"

Optional extra

Explain how labels show the sugar content per 100 grams (see Fact Box). There are five grams in a teaspoon of sugar. Demonstrate how we can work out how many teaspoons are in some food, and spoon the teaspoons onto a plate. This could be extended into an exercise whereby pupils work out how many teaspoons of sugar are in various foods and record their answers onto a grid.

Activity 2

Organise the children into groups. Explain that one child is going to play the part of Great Grandma Toothless and another child is going to be themselves. Great Grandma Toothless is taking the child shopping. Great Grandma Toothless wants to buy a bag of sticky toffee, a bottle of fizzy pop and a bar of chocolate. The group needs to draw or write the shopping list for Great Grandma Toothless to hold. (The items could be varied per group.)

Each group organises a mini-play that shows Great Grandma Toothless walking round the shops, reading her list and about to buy her shopping. Just as she is about to buy something, the child is concerned for Great Grandma's health and decides to encourage her to buy something with less sugar instead. The group needs to decide:

- How do they think both the child and Great Grandma Toothless are feeling at different points of the mini-play?

- What information could the child give to Great Grandma Toothless about sugar?

- What alternatives could the child tell Great Grandma Toothless about?

- How can the child talk to Great Grandma Toothless in a way that is polite and respectful?

- Will Great Grandma Toothless buy what is on her shopping list?

Each group presents their mini-play to the class. Ask the children to evaluate the interactions. "Did the child give Great Grandma Toothless accurate information and alternatives?" "How do you think the child felt at the beginning?" "How did the child talk to Grandma?" "How did Great Grandma react? Why? How do you think Great Grandma felt?" "Why do you think Great Grandma agreed to/didn't agree to change her mind?"

FACT BOX					
Drinks	Quantity	Total sugars content to nearest rounded teaspoon (5 g)*	Confectionery	Quantity	Total sugars content to nearest rounded teaspoon (5 g)*
Cola	330 mls	7			
Fruit juice, ready to drink	300 mls	6	Boiled sweets (large bag)	200 mg	35
	250 mls	5	Kit Kat (4 bar)	48 g	5
Lemonade	330 mls	4	Mars Bar	62.5 g	8
Lucozade	380 mls	11	Milky Way	25 g	1
Ribena (blackcurrant juice drink)	300 mls	7	Milk chocolate bar	49 g	6
	250 mls	6	Smarties (tube)	42 g	6
Sunny Delight	300 mls	6	Snickers	64.5 g	6
	250 mls	5	Twix (2 bar pack)	58 g	6

Food Standards Agency (2002) *McCance and Widdowson's The Composition of Foods*. 6th summary edn., Cambridge: Royal Society of Chemistry

FACT BOX
Tooth decay is caused by ...
high sugar intake
eating sugar frequently, especially between meals
keeping food in the mouth too long, for example, sticky food like toffees
poor care of teeth, for example, not brushing and flossing
inadequate fluoride in the diet

Webb. G. (2002) *Nutrition: A Health Promotion Approach*. London: Arnold

Assessment

Ask each child to complete the sentence, "I eat... (something high in sugar), and I could eat... instead." Children could work in pairs to help one another prepare their answers.

Lesson 9 Foods Containing Fat

Aim: to raise awareness about high fat foods in the diet.

Objectives:

- to know that too much fat is unhealthy

- to practise making food choices and choosing alternative options.

National Curriculum: Sc2/2b; PSHE&Citz/3a,5d; En1/2a; PE/4c

Duration: 60 minutes

Learning Styles: auditory, visual

Skills: problem-solving, creative thinking, information processing, reasoning, evaluation, self-awareness, motivation, empathy, social skills.

Preparation and resources:

- Each child needs a copy of the worksheet Charlie's Choices, a piece of paper and a pencil.

Activity 1

Remind the class about The Balance of Good Health plate made in Lesson 2, or the booklet obtained from the Food Standards Agency, and refer them to the Foods containing Fat group. Explain that today we are going to think about the foods that contain a lot of fat. "What kinds of foods contain a lot of fat? Which foods make your fingers greasy?"

Explain that we need some fat in our food because it helps to keep us warm, it stores up energy for when we need it, it contains some goodies such as vitamins. We get this fat in many of the foods that we eat such as milk, cheese, fish and meat. Olive oil and oily fish are to be encouraged. However, explain that most of us are eating far too much fat in foods such as chocolates, crisps and chips, and we need to eat these in moderation. When we are hungry, we need to think of alternative choices.

Give the children the worksheet Charlie's Choices, and read it out loud.

Charlie's Choices

Charlie rolled over in bed and looked at the clock. It was nine o'clock! "Oh no!" he groaned. He had to get to swimming practice and he was going to be late. He threw on his clothes and ran into the kitchen. Charlie's Mum was eating toast. Charlie opened the cupboard. He knew that he needed to eat if he was going to swim, he needed some energy. Mum pointed to the toast, but he chose the cheese and onion crisps and started munching them as he went through the door. "See you later," he called out.

Charlie licked his greasy fingers and rang his Nana's doorbell. She lived down the road and always took him to swimming on a Saturday. "Would you like to take a banana or a chewy crunch bar for after the swim?" Nana said kindly. Charlie chose the banana. "Thanks Nana," he said and put it in his pocket as they walked.

Nana sat by the pool reading while Charlie and his friends practised their lengths and their dives. Charlie chose to do the extra swimming practice because he wanted to win the cup this year. He was getting better and better. Afterwards Nana asked if Charlie would like a drink with the banana. The café sold cola or milk. Charlie chose cola, and ate his banana.

When he got home Charlie took a digestive biscuit from the biscuit tin, and turned on the TV to watch the cartoons. Dad called out, "Charlie, I'm taking Jasper for his walk. Do you want to come?" "No thanks Dad." Charlie chose to watch the TV.

Soon it was lunchtime. Mum said, "Charlie, shall we have tomato soup and a ham sandwich for lunch or shall we nip out to get some chips?" Charlie chose chips, and ate them with tomato ketchup and salt.

Charlie chose to spend the afternoon playing computer games. At three o'clock he wandered into the kitchen and found some cheese, apples, bread and jam, a king size Mars Bar and packets of smoky bacon crisps. He chose the Mars Bar, and was just swallowing the last mouthful when his friend Mike called round. "Do you want to come out for a bike ride?" Charlie chose to go with Mike. He checked it was okay with his Dad, and returned to the kitchen. Mike and he would need something for the bike ride wouldn't they? He chose the two packets of smoky bacon crisps.

Charlie and his Mum and Dad ate delicious spaghetti bolognaise for tea. It was really yummy. Charlie sat with his clean plate. "Would you like ice cream or fruit salad?" asked Mum. Charlie chose ice cream. They all watched TV. Charlie went to bed, after choosing to eat some of the chocolate Easter egg that he had kept under his bed. What choices had Charlie made that day?

Ask the children to work in pairs and underline all the food choices that Charlie made during the day. You could re-read the story slowly and prompt them, or leave them to do this in pairs.

Draw two columns on the board with headings Charlie's choices and Alternative (or other) choices. Ask the children to copy this down.

Charlie's food choices   **Alternative food choices**

1.

2.

3.

Ask the children to identify three of Charlie's food choices that could have been better, and draw or write them in the left hand column. Can the children think what would have been better choices? Draw or write them in the right hand column. Feed back and discuss as a class.

Many of Charlie's food choices were very high in fat. Also, Charlie was eating too much and too frequently. He wasn't eating enough variety from across the food groups. Draw the children's attention to the Balance of Good Health display. Ask them to consider the overall balance of Charlie's diet throughout the day. "How balanced was his diet? Do you think he ate from all the food groups?"

Remind the class of the work they did about 'Why we eat what we eat?' in Lesson 1. "Why was Charlie eating?"

Activity 2

Remind the class that Charlie made some choices that were not directly about food. Working in pairs, ask the children to identify, "What choices did Charlie make which were good for health and wellbeing?" Share with the class. Acknowledge that Charlie made some positive choices. He was enjoying his swimming club, contributing to the team and working towards the goal of championship. He went cycling and seems to have good relationships with his friends and family.

FACT BOX					
What Charlie ate			**What Charlie could have eaten**		
	fat	sugar		fat	sugar
Cheese and onion crisps (34.5 g)	11.7 g	0.2 g	White toast with margarine (30 g)	4.6 g	1 g
Banana (100 g)	0.3 g	20.9 g	Banana (100 g)	0.3g	20.9 g
Cola (330 mls)	0 g	35.9 g	Milk (200 mls semi-skimmed)	3.4 g	*9.4 g
Digestive biscuit (14 g)	2.8 g	1.9 g	Tomato soup (400 mls)	12 g	10.4 g
Chips (200 g)	24.8 g	3.4 g	Ham sandwich (2 slices of white bread, boiled ham)	1.6 g	3.4 g
King Size Mars Bar	15.5 g	56.3 g	Jam sandwich	0.4 g	1 g

FACT BOX					
Smokey bacon crisps (34.5 g)	11.7 g	0.2 g	Cheese (30 g matchbox size)	17.4 g	0
Spaghetti bolognaise (200 g)	12.3 g	2.6 g	Apple (120 g)	0.1 g	*17.7 g
Ice cream (80 g)	7.8 g	15 g	Spaghetti bolognaise	12.3 g	2.6 g
Milk chocolate (50 g)	15.3 g	28.4 g	Fruit salad (100 g)	0.1 g	*14.4 g
TOTAL	102.2 g	164.8 g		52.2g	80 g

*Milk sugar or fruit sugar eaten within the fruit, as opposed to fruit juice, does not damage teeth.

Assessment

Ask the children to work in small groups. Each child needs to talk about one food choice that they made today or yesterday or 'usually make on a Saturday', and why they made that choice. The group needs to consider what alternative choices could have been made instead, and find out how acceptable this would be to the child. Each group feeds back one of their suggestions to the class.

Lesson 10 What We Eat

Aim: to consolidate learning about The Balance of Good Health within a social context.

Objectives:

- to demonstrate an understanding of a balance using the food groups

- to practise social skills in the context of eating out.

National Curriculum: Sc2/2b; PSHE&Citz/1e,2f,3a,4a,4f,5g

Duration: 80 minutes

Learning Styles: visual, auditory, kinaesthetic

Skills: enquiry, problem-solving, creative thinking, information processing, reasoning, evaluation, self-awareness, managing feelings, motivation, empathy, social skills

Preparation and resources:

- Each child needs a copy of the worksheet Good Health showing a blank Balance of Good Health plate.

- For one of the lower Key Stage 2 activities, each child needs the worksheet A Balanced Meal.

- For one of the upper Key Stage 2 activities, each group of children need a copy of one scenario from the worksheet Solving the Problem.

Activity

Ask the children to work individually or in pairs and draw or write as many foods and drinks as they can think of in the appropriate section of the blank plate in the worksheet Good Health. If they are not sure which food group the food or drink belongs to, they should ask or look at the Balance of Good Health plate displayed.

Remind the children that we should all be eating:

- plenty of the bread, potatoes and other cereals group (eat more)

- plenty of the fruit and vegetables group (moderate amounts)

- a little less meat, fish and alternatives (moderate amounts)

- a little less milk and milk products (moderate amounts)

- foods containing sugar (in moderation, not too frequently)

- foods containing fat (moderate some high fat foods, but encourage oily fish and olive oil).

There are two suggested activities, one for lower Key Stage 2 and another for upper Key Stage 2.

For Lower Key Stage 2

Activity 1

Organise the children into groups of approximately five children. Using the worksheet A Balanced Meal, ask each child to draw a meal on to the plate and a drink by the side. They should include at least one item from each of the four food groups and try to exclude the treats.

Ask the children to swap their papers among the group. Another child is to assess whether the four food groups are represented on the plate. Explain to the children, "If they have included the four food groups, you must praise and congratulate them." "If they have not included the four food groups, make a suggestion about what they could add to the plate and help them to make their meal more balanced."

Activity 2

In order to explore some social and emotional aspects of eating, introduce the theme of eating out in cafes and restaurants. Have any children been to cafés or restaurants with waiters and waitresses? Ask each group to nominate a chef and a waiter/waitress for their group. Ask the class, "What do chefs do?" "What do waiters and waitresses do?" "How can we ask for our food, politely, in a restaurant?" "What do we say when we are given our food in a restaurant?"

Ask each child to remember as much as they can about what they drew on their own plate.

Ask the chef to collect all the group's drawings together.

Ask the waiter to walk up to one child and ask, "What would you like to eat today?" The child requests her own meal. The waiter goes to the chef who finds the correct meal, gives it to the waiter, who serves it to the child. Demonstrate the process in front of the class before the exercise begins.

When each child has been served with their own food, the waiter/waitress and chef can find their own meals.

"Was everyone served the meal that they wanted?" "How did they feel being customers?" "How did the waiter/waitress feel?"

Ask the chef to collect the group's drawings again. Explain to the children that they are going to repeat the activity, but this time the chef has left his glasses at home. He/she can't see very well and is having a very busy day. She/he keeps getting muddled up and giving the waiter/waitress the wrong meal. Each child needs to order his meal as before from the waiter/waitress. Sometimes the waiter/waitress will return with the correct meal, and sometimes they will return with the incorrect meal. If a child is served with the wrong meal they need to (i) explain that the meal is not what they ordered (ii) repeat what they originally ordered and (iii) politely ask the waiter/waitress to correct the mistake. Talk through an example in front of the class. They could practise their responses before the activity begins. When everyone has been served the correct meal, the activity ends.

Put a range of plates on display, showing a good variety of ideas.

Assessment

The children's drawings illustrate their learning of the Balance of Good Health Plate.

For Upper Key Stage 2

Activity 1

Ask the children to work in pairs and draw or write a menu for a breakfast and lunch only, or for the whole day. When thinking about the main course and the dessert, they should try to think about the balance of foods and drinks.

For example, they could be asked to use:

- at least two portions/items from the bread, potatoes and other cereals group
- at least two portions/items from the fruit and vegetables group
- at least one portion/item from the meat, fish and alternatives group
- at least one portion/item from the milk and milk products group.

You might like to draw a template on the board and talk through some examples.

Breakfast	**Lunch**
Weetabix	chicken
milk	baked potato
banana	lettuce and tomato

Ask the children to decorate their menus. Share the menus with the class and display some that show a good variety of ideas.

Activity 2

Introduce the theme of eating out in cafés and restaurants. Have any children been to cafés or restaurants? Ask the children to work in groups and agree on something they all like about eating out, and something they dislike. Share these with the class.

Explain that each group is going to present a mini play about eating out called Solving the Problem. Give each group one of the scenarios written on the worksheet Solving the Problem. Read it through with the group. Each group needs to act out the scenario including their solution.

After each mini play ask the children in the group to explain the reasons for their solution. Ask the other children to evaluate how well the group had dealt with the problem. Encourage the children to think about their feelings and those of others, how to be assertive not aggressive in asking for something, and how they can protect their own and others' self-esteem.

Assessment

The children's menus illustrate their learning of the Balance of Good Health plate.

Comments from educators

"We devised a healthy menu for a day looking at the amounts required in each food group." (Teacher Year 5)

Good Health

A Balanced Meal

Solving the problem

You are in a restaurant.
You and your friends order your lunch. You order a vegetarian meal because you do not eat meat. When the waiter/waitress brings the meal, you are very unhappy because there is ham on the plate. How are you and your friends going to solve the problem?

You are in a self-service café.
You have queued up for ages with your friends, and you are tired. You each choose sandwiches and a drink, and put them on your trays. You pay the person at the till. Just as you are about to sit down, one of you realises that you have not been given the correct change. How are you and your friends going to solve the problem?

You and your friends have bought burgers in a fast food restaurant.
You are walking down the street and chatting. Suddenly one of you bites into the burger to find that it is red and raw in the middle. You know that this could give you food poisoning, but you are so very hungry. How are you and your friends going to solve the problem?

You have made a New Year's resolution that you are going to eat more healthily from now on.
On January 2nd you meet your friends in the local playground. One friend brings a large box of chocolates and another a bumper bag of crisps that they were given for Christmas. You have two chocolates as a treat. You know that you are having a nice meal when you get home, and you don't want to eat any more. You want to try and stick to your New Year's resolution. However, all your friends are tucking in and wondering why you have stopped eating. You are beginning to feel uncomfortable. How are you going to solve the problem?

Your favourite Auntie Molly has invited you and your friends for tea.
You sit at the table and Auntie serves minced beef, potato mash and peas. Everyone is smiling apart from your best friend. He/she is Hindu and can't eat beef. How are you going to solve the problem?

Lesson 11 When We Eat

Aim: to raise awareness about how three regular meals provide energy for daily activities.

Objectives:

- to know that we need food to provide energy for activities throughout the day

- to understand the importance of regular, spaced, eating for health

- to reflect on each child's own eating pattern.

National Curriculum: Sc2/2b; PSHE&Citz/1a,3a; PE/4a

Duration: 60 minutes

Learning Styles: visual, auditory

Skills: information processing, reasoning, evaluation, self-awareness, social skills

Preparation and resources:

- Each child will need a pencil and a long strip of paper that shows a 24 hour time line. This could be made by cutting an A4 piece of paper in half lengthways and sticking the ends together.

- You might like to read Chapter One and Chapter Six.

Activity 1

Distribute the strips to each child and draw the time line on the board alerting them to the times. Ask the children what time they get up in the morning and write 'Get Up' over the appropriate time. Ask the children to copy this on their strips. Continue to ask the children about key moments of the day such as when they have breakfast, lunch, play, go to bed. Write these on the board and ask the children to copy them down.

_____

  6 am 7 am 8 am 9 am 10am 11 am 12 1 pm 2 pm 3 pm 4 pm 5 pm 6 pm 7 pm

Ask the children to draw some pictures of themselves above and along the timeline. For example:

This is me getting up (just before breakfast).

This is me working in class in the morning.

This is me playing at break time.

These should not be coloured in yet.

Ask the children to think about the time of the day when they need energy, and what they need it for. For example, we need energy to do our work in the morning, we need energy to play.

Take a coloured pen and begin to draw an energy line across the strip on the board. The line shows low energy first thing in the morning, and high energy after eating breakfast. Ask the children to copy this down on their own strips using a coloured pen. Encourage the children to think about how energy rises and falls through the day and gradually complete the energy line for the day.

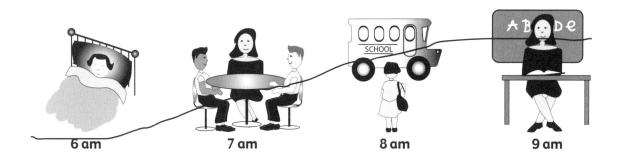

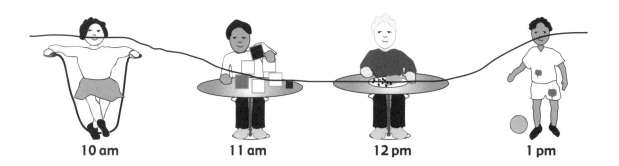

Ask the children to show their time line to another child and explain what the picture shows. "How is your picture different to theirs?" "Why is it different?"

The children can colour in their pictures. Some time lines could be displayed in the classroom.

Optional extra

Show the class what happens to the energy line if we snack continuously all day, and what happens if we miss meals.

Assessment

Ask the children to self-evaluate their eating patterns. How often are they eating? Do they miss meals? How do they feel if they eat too frequently or miss a meal? Ask some of the children to share their thoughts about what they have learnt in groups and then with the class.

Lesson 12 Review and Preparation

Aim: to foster a positive and sensitive culture, with agreed boundaries, within the class.

Objectives:

- to review learning to date
- to set ground rules
- to prepare for Lessons 13 to 19.

National Curriculum: PSHE&Citz/1a,1d,3a,4a,4d,5b,5c.

Duration: 80 minutes.

Learning Styles: visual, auditory.

Skills: visual, auditory, self awareness, creative thinking, information processing, empathy, social skills.

Preparation and resources:

- Each group of children will need a large piece of paper and writing/drawing materials.
- A large piece of paper for the Ground Rules to be displayed.

Activity 1

In order to place children into mixed groups, attribute to each child a positive attribute. "You are great. You are terrific. You are wonderful. You are happy. You are a champion." Ask all the 'champions' to sit with other champions in order to form a group. Repeat for other groups.

Ask the groups to draw or write all that they have learnt about healthier eating onto a large sheet of paper. They could refer to classroom displays and other resources. Ask each group to hold up their poster and tell the rest of the class what they remembered.

Having praised and reviewed any key points of learning, draw the children's attention to some of the social and emotional aspects of the work, reminding them that we all have feelings about what we eat, how we eat and when we eat.

Activity 2

Explain that the next lessons (13 to 19) are going to be focusing on our bodies, how they change and our feelings about this. "Sometimes talking about our bodies can make us feel uncomfortable or embarrassed, so it is important that we all feel comfortable when we do this work. I am suggesting that we agree some ground rules." Explain what ground rules are and give some examples:

- no teasing
- no laughing
- respect everyone is different
- listen.

Ask the children to talk to each other in their groups about what ground rules they would like to set for the class. Ask them to feed back, and write all suggestions on the board. Ask the groups to discuss all the suggestions, and identify the ones to which they would like to agree, and those with which they would have difficulties.

Ask each group to feed back on their discussion. Collate a final list of ground rules onto a large sheet of paper for display. Ask each child to sign the paper. Keep the ground rules on display until all the relevant lessons have been completed.

Assessment

Turn over the paper. How many of the ground rules can each group remember?

Lesson 13 Food and Activity

Aim: to recognise the importance of balancing food intake with activity.

Objectives:

- to explore the physical consequences related to the balancing of food and activity.

- to explore the psychological consequences related to the balancing of food with activity.

National Curriculum: Sc2/2b,2h; PSHE&Citz/3a; PE/4a,4c; A&D/2c

Duration: 60 minutes.

Learning Styles: visual, auditory, kinaesthetic.

Skills: creative thinking, information processing, reasoning, motivation, empathy, social skills.

Preparation and resources:

- You will need a clean board and several board markers for the children.

- Each group of children will need a large piece of modelling material (for example, play dough, modelling clay), and suitable table covering if necessary.

- You will need to refer to the strips from Lesson 11.

Activity

Using the strips from Lesson 11, remind the children of how we use the energy that we get from food and drink for work and play. This is why it is important to eat three good meals each day.

This activity is presented as a whole class activity, but it could be adapted to group work.

Ask some of the children to draw or write an example of the food that they eat on the left hand side of the board. Tell them they have two minutes only! Encourage the class to call out and help the children with ideas. Draw an arrow in the middle of the board.

Ask the children to think of all the ways that they use the energy from this food. "What can you do with your body?" Consider breathing, thinking, walking, skipping, swimming, jumping and so forth. Some activities are more physical, and therefore use our bodies more than others. Ask some children to draw or write physical activities on the right hand side of the board. Tell them they have two minutes only! Encourage the class to call out and help the children with ideas.

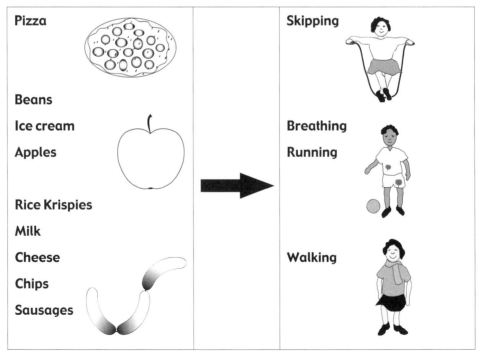

Ask the children to tell you why these activities are good for us. "How are they good for our bodies? How do they make us feel?" Encourage the children to consider the physical (my legs get stronger), social (like playing with friends) and psychological (feel good when I score a goal) benefits of being active. Acknowledge that some children don't like some activities. What do they like to do instead, or what helps to make activities more fun?

Ask the children, "What would happen to my body if I ate all this food (on the left hand side) and didn't do any activities?" Consider getting fatter, slower, weaker, more tired and more out of breath. "How might I feel?"

"What would happen to my body if I did all these activities (on the right hand side) and didn't eat this food?" Consider getting thinner, weaker, more tired and more out of breath. "How might I feel?"

"So what do I need to do to keep my body healthy, strong and active?" Consider the concept of balancing food intake with activity. Emphasise the importance of physical activity.

Assessment

Organise the children into three groups, and ask each group to work together to prepare three 'energy sculptures' using modelling material. The sculptures represent:

- a lot of food and little daily activity

- a little food and a lot of daily activity

- regular intakes of food and regular daily activity.

Let all the children see the sculptures. Ask the groups to explain what they have tried to represent.

Comments from educators

"We didn't have strips from Lesson 11, so we began by calling out everyone's favourite foods and then everyone's favourite activities. The children responded well to this. We also talked about the different types of energy that different food gives us, for example, chocolate might give a short, sharp burst of energy (because of the high sugar content), whereas a banana would give a slower, sustained release of energy. We related this to playing football. I added the question at the end of this session. "Is it better to be too thin or too fat?". This was added because the class teacher had identified a problem with pupils not eating and being underweight. The class discussed how both being underweight and overweight can be bad for your health. Both can stop you being able to do the activities you like, as well as those you might like to do." (School nurse Year 3)

"We referred to the time line from Lesson 11 adapted to our own day, and then linked it to this work on food and activity." (Teacher Year 5)

Lesson 14 Understanding Changes In Body Shape

Aim: to understand how body shape changes are part of healthy growth and development.

Objectives:

- to identify some of the ways that girls' and boys' bodies change shape with age

- to understand some of the reasons why bodies change shape.

National Curriculum: Sc2/2f; PSHE&Citz/3c,5i.

Duration: 50 minutes

Learning Styles: visual, auditory, kinaesthetic.

Skills: information processing, reasoning, self-awareness, social skills.

Preparation and resources:

- You will need a copy of the Information Sheet Body Shape Development age 7-11.

- Each child will need a copy of the worksheet Growing Up.

- You will need to prepare TRUE and FALSE signs.

Activity 1

Ask the children how their bodies have changed since they were small children. Consider how they have grown taller, wider, facial changes and so forth. Consider how their bones give their bodies shape. Ask the children to feel their heads, hand bones, rib cages, leg bones. Ask the children to feel their hips. Explain how girls have a slightly different skeletal shape compared to boys. "Do you know why?" Girls usually have wider hips ready for when they might give birth to a baby when they are women. Ask the children to put both their hands on the shoulders of the child next to them. "Can you feel the shoulder tips?" Boys usually have slightly wider shoulders ready for the muscles that will develop later, for strong upper body strength.

Explain how the body changes some of their food into fat that is stored under their skins. Ask the children to pinch the fat on their arms. Can they feel it? Explain that the fat under their skin keeps them warm and makes their body change shape as they grow. The body stores fat inside the body to protect organs as well. The body cleverly stores fat as part of growing into a healthy adult.

Activity 2

Give each child a copy of the worksheet Growing Up and talk the children through how body shape develops differently for girls and boys using the Information Sheet Body Shape Development age 7-11 for guidance.

Assessment

Put a True and False sign in each corner of the room. Read out the following statements and ask the children to work as a pair, and move quietly, or to point, to the appropriate corner of the room.

True or False

- Girls' and boys' bodies are growing and changing all the time. (T)

- Boys have wider hips than girls because boys will need to be able to give birth to babies. (F)

- By about nine many girls begin to grow quite fast. (T)

- Most boys start to grow fast once they go to secondary school. (T)

- At about nine it is normal and healthy for boys to start feeling a little fatter around their tummies because they are going to grow up to be women. (F)

- At about nine it is normal and healthy for girls to start feeling a little fatter around their tummies because they are going to grow up to be women. (T)

- When girls go to secondary school, they will start to develop very muscly legs and arms, more than boys. (F)

- By the time girls leave primary school some will have more fat on their thighs, upper arms and breasts because their bodies are changing into women. (T)

Comments from educators

"The class greatly enjoyed the True and False statements, and seemed to appreciate the break in concentration." (School nurse Year 3)

Information Sheet

Body Shape Development age 7-11

Children's Weight And Growth

- Children have gained weight over the last 30 years.

- Today there are slightly more overweight children than underweight children in the UK.

Girls and boys go through similar patterns of growth until they are eight, thereafter the bodily changes for each sex, in terms of character and timing, are distinctly different.

Girls

- Girls have relatively wider hips compared to shoulder breadth in preparation for later childbirth.

- Girls have more subcutaneous fat, that is fat under the skin that affects appearance, than boys at all ages from infancy to 18 years.

- At six or seven years old girls show a slight reduction in this fat before it increases again.

- At nine, just before girls enter puberty, they begin to grow rapidly. This is called the adolescent growth spurt.

- Puberty starts at about ten years old, which is earlier than ever and probably due to improved nutrition. This coincides with an increase in body fat that is related to ensuring the body is ready for menarche.

- Today, in the West, menarche usually occurs from 11 years old.

- Putting on extra fat at about nine years old is part of girls' normal and healthy development.

Boys

- Boys have relatively wider shoulders compared to hips ready to shoulder the upper body's increased muscularity to come.

- Boys have less subcutaneous fat than girls throughout childhood and their teenage years.

- Like girls they experience a slight reduction in fat between six and seven and then it increases again, but does not catch up with the girls.

- The boys' adolescent growth spurt followed by puberty occurs at around 12 to 13 years.

- Like girls they experience increased fat just before puberty, but this is when they have entered secondary school.

In the final years of primary schools girls who have entered puberty have twice as much body fat as boys.

Implications of Girls' and Boys' Differing Body Shapes

- The way that fat is distributed around the body is similar for both girls and boys in childhood.

- At nine both have more fat on their tummies than limbs. With the onset of puberty both gain more fat on their tummies.

- At around nine girls will start to feel fat around their tummies, and boys will feel this at 12 to 13.

- With puberty, girls will begin to experience fat on their thighs, upper arms and breasts.

This means that in the final years of primary school girls are moving towards increased fatness and the development of a rounded shape whereas the boys have not yet begun the move towards increased muscularity and leanness which characterises their adolescence. So it is not surprising that girls, to a greater extent than boys, start to demonstrate an awareness of their changing bodies in later primary school. Whether they have negative or positive views about these changes relates to what they are learning about acceptable and unacceptable body shapes around them.

Summary

By the middle of Key Stage 2 girls and boys are experiencing different changes in their bodies. They both have different body shapes. Whilst girls aspire to be thinner, they are getting unavoidably fatter. Whilst boys fear thinness, their muscles stubbornly wait to develop. Their own weight can influence how they feel, as can perceptions about their peers' bodies and body images in the wider society. In the final year of primary school many girls will be experiencing their pubertal growth spurt, their first periods and related bodily changes such as pubic hair growth, increased perspiration and breast development. Some boys might be concerned that their bodies are not developing. About half of nine year olds are dissatisfied with their body image (Hill et al., 1992; Hill et al., 1992a; Robinson, 1999).

There are many useful resources for teaching children about their bodies and healthy development, though few discuss body shape. Here are some examples.

Cole, B. (2001) *Hair in Funny Places,* London, Jonathan Cape Ltd.

Harris, R.H. (1995) *Let's Talk about Sex Growing up, Changing Bodies, Sex and Sexual Health*, London, Walker Books.

Madaras, L. (2000) *What's Happening to My Body? Book for Boys: A Growing up Guide for Parents and Sons*, New York, Newmarket Press.

Madaras, L. (2003) *Ready, Set Grow! A What's Happening to My Body? Book for Younger Girls*, New York, Newmarket Press.

Swinden, L. (1990) *Knowing Me, Knowing You. Strategies for Sex Education in the Primary School,* Wisbech, LDA.

Royston, A. (1993) *What's Inside My Body*, London, Dorling Kindersley.

Willis, J. (2004) *Bits, Boobs and Blobs*, London, Walker Books.

One of the few resources that addresses changing body shape, along with feelings and eating, is the Eating Disorders Association's web site: www.edauk.com.

Growing Up

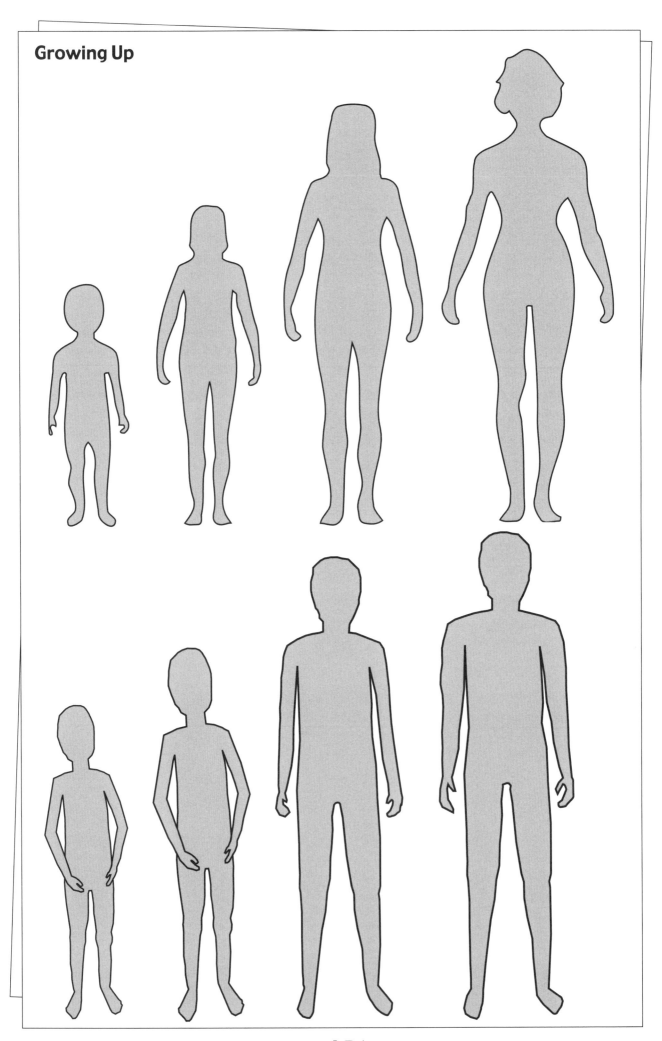

Lesson 15 My Changing Body

Aim: to allow children to prepare for their body shape changes as they grow.

Objectives:

- to identify some specific changes in the children's bodies since birth

- to appreciate that everybody is unique and very capable.

National Curriculum: Sc2/2f; PSHE&Citz/3c,5b,5i

Duration: 50 minutes.

Learning Styles: visual, auditory, kinaesthetic.

Skills: reasoning, creative thinking, self-awareness, social skills.

Preparation and resources:

- Each child needs a piece of paper and a pencil or crayon.

Activity 1

Draw a large hand on the board. Label the hand as shown below. Leave plenty of space around the hand.

Ask the children to draw round their own hands, or ask a friend to draw around their hand, and copy the labels from the board.

Explain that we are going to think about some of the wonderful things that our bodies can do. Tell the children about something that your body could do when you were one year old (for example, breathing, drinking). Write this by the drawing of the thumb on the board. Then tell the class of something wonderful your body could do when you were three years old (walking, talking), and write this near the index finger.

Explain that the children are going to draw or write around their own hands. They should think of two things that their body could do at one year, at three years, at five years and this year. By the little finger they should draw or write two things that their body is going to be, or be able to do, next year. You could give some examples such as, "Do you think that you will be smaller, taller, thinner, fatter?" "Do you think you will be able to run faster?"

Collect and share some examples of children's work and discuss how our bodies have always been changing and developing. This has been necessary in order to be able to do what we want to do as we get older. "Aren't we glad that our bodies changed, so that we can run faster and so forth?" Make links to the work on healthy body development.

Activity 2

Mix up all the children's labelled hands and redistribute them so that they do not receive their own. Organise the children to work in groups. Ask the group to consider, "Are our hands the same or are they different? Look at all the different shapes and sizes of hands." Allow the groups to feed back what they have observed to each other and then the class.

"Have a look at your own fingers and have a look at someone else's. Have a look at the colour, shape and size. Have a close look at their fingerprints." Allow the children to share what they have observed with each other and then the class.

Re-enforce that even our fingerprints are all different. "Yet, despite the differences, we can still do lots of things with our hands. What are all the wonderful things that we can do with our hands?" Ask each group to think of as many things as possible. Ask each group to mime something that we can do with our hands to the class. Can the class guess what it is?

Summarise by reminding the children that our bodies, like our hands, are unique and always changing. They are changing so that we can continue to do all those wonderful things with them. Display some of the children's drawings of hands.

Assessment

"Next year our bodies are all going to have changed. Let's see if we can remember six things that we said."

Comments from educators

"Worked well for all abilities. Enjoyed remembering what they could do when younger. Found it hard to predict for the following year. Excellent for thinking about physical development. Could extend easily to social ideas also." (Teacher Year 5)

Optional Extra – Circle Time

Ask the children to sit in a circle. Each child is asked to complete the sentence.

My name is … and the person on my right is …

My hands can …

My body can …

The best thing about my body is …

My body feels …

Next year my body will change. It will be …

This makes me feel …

My body feels really good when …

Lesson 16 Thinking About How People Feel

Aim: to explore feelings associated with being teased, and teasing others, about their size.

Objectives:

- to feel empathy towards another
- to practise the language of empathic communication
- to practise evaluation of the children's own work
- to practise team work.

National Curriculum: PSHE&Citz/4a,4d,4e; En1/4a,4b

Duration: 80 minutes.

Learning Styles: visual, auditory, kinaesthetic

Skills: enquiry, problem-solving, creative thinking, reasoning, evaluation, self-awareness, managing feelings, empathy, social skills

Preparation and resources:

- You and/or the children will need the worksheet Josh's First Day at a New School.

Activity 1

Explain that the lesson is going to be looking at teasing. "What do you think about teasing?" "Is it nice to tease people?" "What kind of things do children tease other children about?" "How does it feel to be teased? Do you know? Can you imagine?"

Suggestions for how the worksheet Josh's First Day at a New School could be used include:

- Children could be given the story to read and asked to draw or write inside the bubbles, working in pairs or in groups.
- You could read the story aloud in stages, and encourage groups of children to decide what they would like to draw or write inside the bubbles.
- The story could be read aloud, and the children could be encouraged to think about a response in their groups. After a time limit, each group could call out responses, and discuss them as a class.
- You might like to vary the story according to the children's needs.

Activity 2

Ask the children to agree upon a dialogue and present the story as a mini play. This could be done in two or more groups. Children could be asked to develop the story further.

Provide time for the children to rehearse their mini-play. Encourage the children to evaluate and question their work. Explore any issues which arise.

Comments from educators

"Group enjoyed the story and could identify with it. It suited all abilities. Some were unsure about explaining the feelings of others, quite a new concept for them. I asked the children to put themselves in a similar situation. Excellent for identifying different feelings." (Teacher Year 5)

Josh's First Day at a New School

Josh and his family have moved to a new house, and today is Josh's first day at his new school. How do you think Josh is feeling?

After lunch three boys come up to Josh. They tease him about the way he looks, his weight and his size. Josh says nothing. How do you think Josh is feeling?

When the boys are teasing Josh, how does this make them feel?

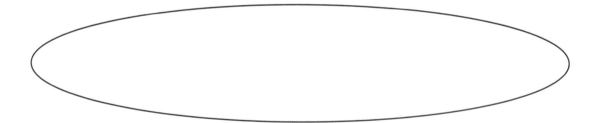

Jack is with some friends on the other side of the playground. Jack plays football for the school. He scored the most goals this season. Jack sees Josh standing alone and looking down at his feet. What do you think Jack is thinking?

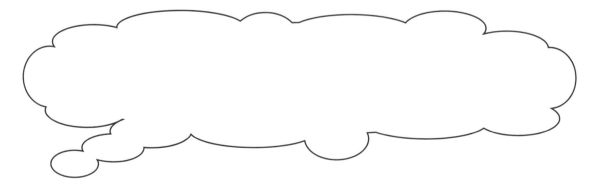

Jack comes to say hello to Josh. Jack wonders who Josh is, what he likes and why he has come to this school. What kind of questions could Jack ask Josh?

Jack finds out that Josh has a dog and two sisters. He changed schools because his Dad got a new job. He likes drawing, playing computer games and football. Jack tells Josh that he likes football too. Jack smiles. How do you think Josh is feeling now?

Jack and Josh walk across the playground towards the three boys. The three boys are sniggering and pointing at Josh. What does Jack say to Josh?

What do Jack and Josh say to the three boys?

How do you think Josh feels now?

How do you think the three boys feel now?

Lesson 17 Experiencing How People Feel

Aim: To build on Lesson 16 and evaluate mini-plays about feelings.

Objectives:

- to practise the language of empathic communication
- to explore feelings and their associated behaviours
- to practise giving sensitive and constructive feedback to others.

National Curriculum: n1/4a,4b,4d

Duration: 60 to 80 minutes

Learning Styles: visual, auditory, kinaesthetic

Skills: creative thinking, evaluation, managing feelings, empathy, social skills

Preparation and resources:

- Prepare the classroom so that there is space for a performance and an audience.

Activity 1

Allow the children a final rehearsal of their mini-play about teasing, based on the scenario in the worksheet Josh's First Day at a New School, or work arising from it.

Activity 2

Explain that each group is going to perform their mini-play to the class. After each performance the children will be working in pairs and discussing what they liked about the play and any suggestions that would make the play better. Also, the actors will be asked how they thought their performance went.

After each performance allow for the reflections and feedback. Some suggestions for improvement could be tried out.

Assessment

"Next time you hear someone being teased about the way they look, what are you going to say and do?" Ask the children to work in pairs and feed back their answers to the class.

Lesson 18 Thinking About Weight Change

Aim: to appreciate the range of reasons which can lie behind different body shapes.

Objectives: to identify specific contributory factors that cause weight loss and weight gain

National Curriculum: PE/4a,4c; PSHE&Citz/3a,4a,4b,4d,4e

Duration: 40 minutes

Learning Styles: visual, auditory

Skills: problem-solving, reasoning, evaluation, empathy, social skills

Preparation and resources:

- Each group of children will need a copy of the worksheet Weight Changes.

- Discussing weight gain and weight loss can be a very sensitive issue. This lesson, along with Lessons 13,14,15,16 and 17, aim to provide factual information to combat misunderstandings that can fuel bullying, teasing or low self-esteem, and to support those feeling vulnerable. You should look at these five lessons together, along with Lesson 12, and consider changing the order if necessary, to best suit the needs of your pupils.

- Approximately six metres of plain or lining wallpaper, ready to be attached to a wall.

Activity 1

Distribute the worksheet Weight Changes showing four children. Explain that one boy and one girl are gaining weight; one boy and one girl are losing weight. Ask the children to work in pairs and consider all the reasons why the children might be gaining or losing weight. They should draw or write their best answers onto the picture of each child (two reasons for weight loss and two reasons for weight gain).

Ask for a boy and girl to volunteer to be drawn around. With the help of a teaching assistant, draw around each child onto a strip of wallpaper to produce two full size templates. Display these on a wall. You might like to add an additional plain strip between the two templates.

Draw a vertical line down the centre of each template body. One side will represent reasons for weight loss, and the other reasons for weight gain.

Ask the children to read out their thoughts recorded on the worksheet. Discuss and write on the girl templates. Challenge any over-simplistic explanations and use the Fact Box to encourage the children to think very broadly.

To summarise, encourage the children to remember that there are lots of reasons why we eat what we eat (Lesson 1), and lots of reasons why people love or sometimes don't like activities (Lesson 13). Our eating and our activity can make a difference to our body size. However, there are wider issues also, and some of these we have no choice about e.g. the genetic make-up of our family and illness, and some we might have little choice about, for example, family lifestyles, the environment in which we live, though these might be changed in time.

FACT BOX	
Reasons for thinness	**Reasons for fatness**
Thin family (genetic)	Fat family (genetic)
Not eating enough for activity needs – missing meals, eating very small portions	Eating too much for activity needs – eating too frequently, too large portions
Excessive activity	Insufficient activity
Illness – mental or physical	Illness – mental or physical
Loss of appetite due to physical, social or emotional factors	Comfort eating due to physical, social or emotional factors
Family eating and activity habits	Family eating and activity habits
Easy access to activity areas e.g. playground	Poor access to activity areas
Poor access to a variety of foods and drinks	Easy access to fast food/snack outlets
Lack of knowledge or skills about healthy eating and activity	Poor access to wide variety of foods – transport, cost
	Lack of knowledge or skills about healthy eating and activity.

Assessment

Ask the children to evaluate their work on the worksheet Weight Changes. Can they add any more reasons to the pictures, which were not there before?

Comments from educators

"Overall the group were able to identify the relationship between food, activity and body size and able to identify reasons beyond this for why people might be the shape they are. I think older children would be able to contribute more. The writing skills in the class varied so, for some, the writing was quite challenging. We concluded the session with the story and questions from Lesson 19 which seemed to summarise this work quite well." (School nurse, Year 3)

Weight Changes

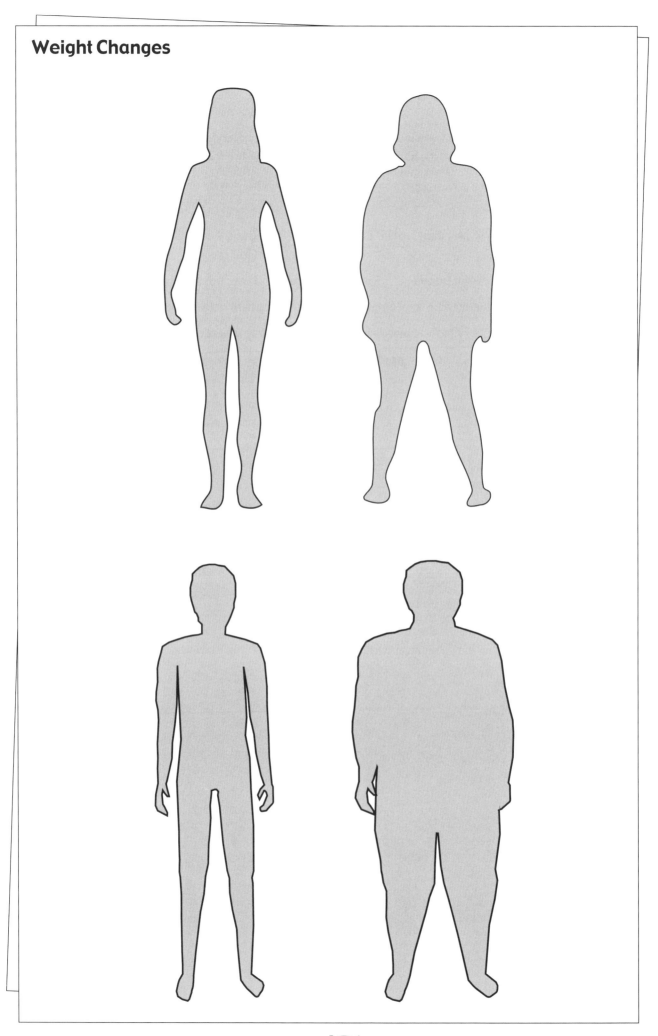

Lesson 19 Feelings, Food and Activity

Aim: to apply previous learning about feelings, food and activity and relate these to a holistic approach to health and happiness.

Objectives:

- to understand why missing meals is unhealthy
- to practise understanding the feelings of others
- to reflect on the factors which can maintain and improve children's own health and wellbeing.

National Curriculum: PSHE&Ciz/3a; PE/4c

Duration: 90 minutes

Learning Styles: visual, auditory, kinaesthetic.

Skills: enquiry, problem-solving, creative thinking, reasoning, self-awareness, empathy, social skills.

Preparation and resources:

- You will need the worksheet Jessica Joins the Dance Class. Alternatively, you may want the children to have their own copies.
- Each group of children will need a very large piece of paper.
- All the children will need crayons.

Activity 1

Read through the story of Jessica Joining the Dance Class. Ask the children to work in groups. "Why do you think Jessica was able to continue dancing the longest?" Allow the groups time to discuss, and agree upon an answer before feeding back to the class. Repeat, for the following questions. "Why do you think Penny and Lucy felt dizzy and out of breath?" "How do you think dancers and pop singers keep themselves healthy so that they can dance well?"

Remind the children about the Balance of Good Health, the importance of three good meals a day and not too many treats, the importance of regular safe physical activity and all the other things that help us to feel happy and well.

Activity 2

Organise the children into groups with a very large piece of paper per group. Ask the children to each draw a picture of themselves dancing or another physical activity that they enjoy onto the paper.

Encourage the groups to discuss all the things that keep them active, happy and healthy. "What do you do to keep yourself active, happy and healthy?" These things should be written and drawn on the paper around the drawings of active children. The group need to work co-operatively to decide what is to be added, where and who is going to write or draw it. When they have finished, each group nominates one child to be their 'expert'. This child remains with the group's drawings.

Explain that all the children, except the 'expert' representatives, are going to walk quietly around the room and look at the other groups' drawings. The children need to work in pairs to think of a question about the drawings to ask the 'expert'. The 'expert's' role is to answer questions.

Display a variety of the pictures.

Assessment

Join the children in looking at each group's drawings. Assess the children's learning from the drawings and through asking the 'expert' questions.

Jessica Joins the Dance Class

Jessica joined the dance class. When she arrived the other children were talking in a corner. Lucy was standing in front of the mirror saying how pleased she was that she hadn't eaten breakfast for a week. Penny boasted that she hadn't eaten lunch and patted her tummy. When Jessica walked in the children looked at her in surprise. "She doesn't look like a dancer," they whispered, "She looks really clumsy and heavy." They laughed. How do you think Jessica feels?

_____

_____

_____

_____

The teacher welcomed Jessica to the class. She turned on the music and started to go through the routine. The children followed the steps to the music. How do you think they were feeling?

_____

_____

_____

_____

_____

After ten minutes Lucy and Penny started to feel dizzy and out of breath. They had to sit down on the floor. Jessica followed the teacher's high kicks and twirls. Jessica clapped her hands in time to the music. The teacher smiled. "Can anyone do this?" she asked as she jumped into the air. Jessica jumped higher than anyone else. Lucy and Penny started to think how wrong they had been. Jessica was great. She had lots of energy. Jessica carried on dancing right to the end of the song. How do you think Jessica feels now?

_____

_____

_____

_____

Examples of Weekly Planning Sheets

Year 4 First Half of Summer Term

Week One

Lesson 1 Why Do We Eat What We Eat

Aim: to highlight that people eat for a wide variety of reasons.

Objectives:

- to identify a wide range of reasons for children's own eating behaviour
- to provide a poster 'Why do we eat what we eat?' for the display board.

Preparation and resources for main activities:

- Each child might need a piece of paper and pencil
- Large sheet of paper for display.

Week Two

Lesson 2 Introducing Food Groups

Aim: to introduce The Balance of Good Health food groups.

Objectives:

- to know that foods can be grouped into food groups
- to identify examples of which foods belong to which group, including those that belong to more than one group
- to produce a large Balance of Good Health plate for display.

Preparation and resources for main activities:

- Each child needs to bring two or three different types of clean packaging from food or drink, such as cans, boxes, wrappers, plastic containers for salad or vegetables and plastic bottles, into school. You might like to collect some additional examples in order to broaden the range.
- Whiteboard pens in colours: orange, green, pink/red, blue, yellow are optional.
- Large labels will be needed for each food group: a set for the display board, and a set for the assessment. (Fruit and vegetables, Bread, other cereals and potatoes, Meat, fish and alternatives, Milk and dairy foods, Foods containing fat, Foods containing sugar.)
- Prepare a giant (as large as possible) blank plate segmented to represent The Balance of Good Health for the display board. See the poster included on the CD-ROM. Either cut up large pieces of coloured paper (orange, green, pink/ red, blue, yellow) ready to be stuck onto the plate's segments or consider another method for quick colouring in.
- Prepare materials for children to draw, paint or make foods.
- Local Health Promotion Departments might be able to loan plastic foods and Balance of Good Health resources.
- An A3 copy of the worksheet Good Health showing a blank Balance of Good Health and small sized food wrappers for each pair of children is optional.

Week Three

Lesson 3 What Are We Eating?

Aim: to begin to understand the importance of eating a variety of foods and a balance of foods for healthy eating.

Objectives:

- to reflect on children's own diets
- to be able to allocate children's own food and drink to the appropriate food groups
- to know that it is important to eat a variety of foods from different food groups.

Preparation and resources for main activities:

- An A4 booklet, *The Balance of Good Health* is available from the Food Standards agency (telephone 0845 6060667, e mail: foodstandards@ecologistics.co.uk) or through your local Health Promotion Department (optional).
- Each child needs a copy of the worksheet What I've Eaten Since Home Time Yesterday and a pencil.
- It is advisable to write a letter to parents and carers explaining the purpose of this work in advance, and to allay any anxieties that they might have.
- The day before, explain to the children, "Tomorrow we are going to look again at what we are all eating. When you go home after school I'd like you to write down everything that you eat and drink until you come back to school tomorrow."

Week Four

Lesson 10 What We Eat

Aim: to consolidate learning about the Balance of Good Health within a social context.

Objectives:

- to demonstrate an understanding of a balance using the food groups
- to practise social skills in the context of eating out.

Preparation and resources:

- Each child needs a copy of the worksheet Good Health showing a blank Balance of Good Health plate.
- Each child needs the worksheet A Balanced Meal.

Week Five

Lesson 11 When We Eat

Aim: to raise awareness about how three regular meals provide energy for daily activities.

Objectives:

- to know that we need food to provide energy for activities throughout the day
- to understand the importance of regular, spaced, eating for health
- to reflect on each child's own eating pattern.

Preparation and resources for main activities:

- Each child will need a long strip of paper which shows a 24 hour time line. This could be made by cutting an A4 piece of paper in half lengthways and sticking the ends together.

Year 6 Second Half of Summer Term

Week 1

Lesson 12 Review and Preparation

Aim: to foster a positive and sensitive culture, with agreed boundaries, within the class.

Objectives:

- to review learning to date
- to set ground rules
- to prepare for Lessons 13 to 19

Preparation and resources for main activities:

- Each group of children will need a large piece of paper and writing/drawing materials.
- A large piece of paper for the Ground Rules to be displayed.

Week 2

Lesson 14 Understanding Changes in Body Shape

Aim: to understand how body shape changes are part of healthy growth and development.

Objectives:

- to identify some of the ways that girls' and boys' bodies change shape with age
- to understand some of the reasons why bodies change shape.

Preparation and resources for main activities:

- You will need a copy of Information Sheet Body Shape Development age 7-11.
- Each child will need a copy of the worksheet Growing Up.
- You will need to prepare TRUE and FALSE signs.

Week 3

Lesson 15 My Changing Body

Aim: to allow children to prepare for their body shape changes as they grow.

Objectives:

- to identify some specific changes in the children's bodies since birth
- to appreciate that everybody is unique and very capable.

Preparation and resources for main activities:

- Each child needs a piece of paper and a pencil or crayon.

Week 4

Lesson 16 Thinking About How People Feel

Aim: to explore feelings associated with being teased, and teasing others, about their size.

Objectives:

- to feel empathy towards another
- to practise the language of empathic communication
- to practise evaluation of the children's own work
- to practise team work.

Preparation and resources for main activities:

- You and/or the children will need the worksheet Josh's First Day at a New School.

Week 5

Lesson 17 Experiencing How People Feel

Aim: to perform and evaluate mini-plays about feelings.

Objectives:

- to practise the language of empathic communication
- to explore feelings and their associated behaviours
- to practise giving sensitive and constructive feedback to others.

Preparation and resources for main activities:

- Prepare the classroom so that there is space for a performance and the audience.

Week 6

Lesson 18 Thinking About Weight Change

Aim: to appreciate the range of reasons which can lie behind different body shapes.

Objectives:

- to identify specific contributory factors which cause weight loss and weight gain.

Preparation and resources for main activities:

- Each group of children will need a copy of the worksheet Weight Changes.
- Approximately five metres of plain or lining wallpaper, ready to be attached to a wall.
- Discussing weight gain and weight loss can be a very sensitive issue. This lesson, along with Lessons 13, 14, 15, 16 and 17 aims to provide factual information to combat misunderstandings that can fuel bullying, teasing or low self-esteem, and to support those who are feeling vulnerable. You should look at these five lessons together, along with Lesson 12, and consider changing the order if necessary, to best suit the needs of their pupils.

References

Baranowski, T., Domel, S., Gould, R., Baranowski, J., Leonard, S., Triber, F. and Mullis, R. (1993) Increasing Fruit and Vegetable Consumption among 4th and 5th Grade Students: Results from Focus Groups using Reciprocal Determinism, *Journal of Nutrition Education*, Vol 25, (iii) 114-120.

Bee, H. (1995) *The Developing Child*, 7th edition, Harper Collins College Publishers, New York.

Birch, L.L. (1991) Obesity and Eating Disorders: A Developmental Perspective, *Bulletin of the Psychonomic Society*, 29, 265-272.

Birch, L. and Marlin, D. (1982) I Don't Like It; I Never Tried It: Effects of Exposure on Two-Year Old Children's Food Preferences, *Appetite Journal for Intake Research, Vol 3*, 353-360.

Blinkhorn, A.S. Roberts, B.P. and Duxbury, J.T. (2003) The Ability of Young Children to Influence Adults in the Choice of Sugary Foods and Drinks, *Health Education Journal*, Vol 62, (iii) 210-219.

Blissett, J., Lysons, T. and Norman, P. (1996) Dieting Behaviour and Views of Young Children in Wales, *Health Education Journal*, Vol 55, (i) 101-107.

Bryant-Waugh, R. (2000) Overview of Eating Disorders. In Last, B. and Bryant-Waugh, R. 2000 *Anorexia Nervosa and Related Eating Disorders in Childhood and Adolescence, 2nd edn*, Hove, Psychology Press Ltd.

Chapiti, U., Jean-Marie, S. and Chan, W. (2000) Cultural and Religious Influences on Adult Nutrition in the UK, *Nursing Standard*, Vol 14 (29) 47-51.

Charles, N., Kerr, M. (1988) *Women, Food and Families*, Manchester University Press, Manchester.

Clayton, B. and Fewell, A. (1998) *What are Today's Children Eating? The Gardner Merchant School Meals Survey 1998*. Kenley, Gardner Merchant Ltd.

Cline, S. (1990) *Just Desserts: Women and Food*, London, Andre Deutsch Ltd.

Co-op (2000) *Blackmail: The First in a Series of Inquiries into Consumer Concerns about the Ethics of Modern Food Production and Advertising*, Manchester, CWS Ltd.

Cole, T.J., Freeman, J.V. and Preece, M.A. (1995) Body Mass Index Reference Curves for the UK, 1990, *Archives of Disease in Childhood, Vol 73*, 25-29.

Conner, M.T., Bell, R. and Grogan, S.C. (1991) Gender Differences in Attitudes Towards Eating Sweet Snack Foods, *Paper presented at the British Feeding and Drinking Group*, Sheffield, April 8-9th.

Cristofoli, A., Howse, A., Mbofana, D., Townsend, C., and Tutchell, E. (1997) *Body Image Healthy Eating and Young People. An Information and Activity Pack for Teachers and Youth Workers*, Berkshire Health Promotion, University of Reading.

Crisp, A.H. (1988) Some Possible Approaches to the Prevention of Eating and Body Weight/Shape Disorders, With Particular Reference to Anorexia Nervosa. *International Journal of Eating Disorders, Vol 7*, (i) 1-17.

Crockett, S.J. and Sims, L.S. (1995) Environmental Influences on Children's Eating, *Journal of Nutrition Education, Vol 27*, (v) 235-249.

Davison, K.K. and Birch, L.L. (2001) Childhood Overweight: A Contextual Model and Recommendations for Future Research. *The International Association for the Study of Obesity. Obesity Reviews, Vol 2*, 159-171.

Dawson, D. (1995) *Eating Disorders. A Quick Guide*, Cambridge, Daniels Publishing.

Denman, S., Moon, A., Parsons, C. and Stears, D. (2001) *The Health Promoting School. Policy, Research and Practice*, London, Routledge.

Department for Education and Employment/Qualifications and Curriculum Authority (1999) *The National Curriculum. Handbook for Primary Teachers. Key Stages 1 and 2*, London, HMSO.

Department for Education and Employment (1999) *National Healthy School Standard. Getting Started – A Guide for Schools*, London, DfEE.

Department for Education and Skills (2003) *Primary National Strategy. Developing Children's Social, Emotional and Behavioural Skills Guidance*, London, DfES.

Department for Education and Skills (2004a) *Healthy Living Blueprint for Schools,* London, DfES.

Department for Education and Skills (2004b) *Primary National Strategy. Excellence and Enjoyment: Learning and Teaching in the Primary Years, Understanding how Learning Develops.* London, DfES.

Department for Education and Skills (2004c) *Establishing a Whole-school Food Policy*, London, DfES.

Department for Education and Skills/Department of Health (2004) *Promoting Emotional Health and Wellbeing through the National Healthy School Standard*, London, DoH/DfES.

Department for Education and Skills/Focus on Food (2003) *Establishing a Food Partnership between Primary and Secondary Schools*, London, DfES/British Nutrition Foundation/The Design and Technology Association.

Department for Education and Skills/Food Standards Agency (2004) *Starting Early: Food and Nutrition Education of Young Children* HMI 2292, London, Ofsted

Department of Health (1991) *Report on Health and Social Subjects 41: Dietary Reference Values for Food Energy and Nutrients for the United Kingdom*, London, HMSO.

Department of Health (1994) *Report on Social Subjects No.46: Nutritional Aspects of Coronary Heart Disease*, London, HMSO.

Department of Health (1998) *Nutritional Aspects of the Development of Cancer (COMA)*, London, The Stationery Office.

Department of Health (1989) *Dietary Sugars and Human Disease*, London, HMSO.

Department of Health (2003) *Annual Report of the Chief Medical Officer 2002*, London, The Stationery Office.

Department of Health (2004a) *The National School Fruit Scheme*, London, DoH.

Department of Health (2004b) *Choosing Health. Making Healthier Choices Easier*, London, DoH.

Department of Health (2004c) *National Service Framework for Children, Young People and Maternity Services*, London, Department of Health.

Department of Health (2005) *Choosing a Better Diet. A Food and Health Action Plan*, London, DoH.

Department of Education and Skills/Department of Health (2005) *The National Healthy School Status. A Guide for Schools.* London, DoH.

Dibb, S. (1993) *Children: Advertisers' Dream, Nutrition Nightmare?* London, National Food Alliance.

Dieter, W. and Skuse, D. (1992) Management of Infant Feeding Problems. In Cooper, P.J. and Stein, A. 1992 *Feeding Problems and Eating Disorders in Children and Adolescents*, Reading, Harwood, 27-59.

Dixey, R., Sahota, P., Atwal, S., Turner, A. (2001) *"Ha Ha, You're Fat, We're Strong"; A Qualitative Study of Boys' and Girls' Perceptions of Fatness, Thinness, Social Pressures and Health using Focus Groups, Health Education, Vol 101*, (v) 206-216.

Dixey, R., Sahota, P., Atwal, S. and Turner, A. (2001a) *Children Talking about Healthy Eating: Data from Focus Groups with 300 9-11-Year Olds, British Nutrition Foundation, Nutrition Bulletin, Vol 26*, 71-79.

Doyle, M. and Hosfield, N. (2003) *Health Survey for England 2001: Fruit and Vegetable Consumption*, London, The Stationery Office.

Eating Disorders Association (2002) *It's Not About Food... It's About Feelings*, Norwich, EDA.

Edelman, B. (1982) Developmental Differences in the Conceptualization of Obesity, *Journal of the American Dietetic Association, Vol 80*, 122-127.

Falciglia, G.A., Couch, S.C., Gribble, L.S., Pabst, S.M. and Frank, R. (2000) Food Neophobia in Childhood Affects Dietary Variety, *Journal of the American Dietetic Association, Vol 100*, (xii) 1474-1481.

Florey, L. (2004) *Understanding Eating Distress*, Manchester, MIND.

Fredricks, A.M., Van Buuren, S., Wit, J.M. and Verloove-Vanhorick, S.P. (2000) Body Index Measurement in 1996-7 Compared with 1980, *Archives of Disease in Childhood*, 82, 107 112.

Freeman, J.V., Cole, T.J., Chinn, S., Jones, P.R.M., White, E.M. and Preece, M.A. (1995) Cross Sectional Stature and Weight Reference Curves for the UK, 1990, *Archives of Diseases in Childhood*, 73, 17-24.

Food Standards Agency (2001) *The Balance of Good Health*, London, FSA.

Forrester, H. (2002) *A Draft Report of the Published Scientific Literature on the Impacts of Water on Health*, Water UK.

Gallway, A.T., Lee, Y. and Birch, L. (2003) Predictors and Consequences of Food Neophobia and Pickiness in Young Girls, *Journal of the American Dietetic Association*, Vol 103, (vi) 692-698.

Garner, D. and Garfinkel, P. (1980) Cultural Expectations of Thinness in Women, *Psychological Reports, Vol 47*, 483-491.

Garrow, J.S. (1988) *Obesity and Related Diseases*, Churchill Livingstone, London.

Gregory, J., Foster, K., Tyler, H. and Wiseman, M. (1990) *The Dietary and Nutritional Survey of British Adults: A Survey of the Dietary Behaviour, Nutritional Status and Blood Pressure of Adults aged 16 to 64 living in Great Britain*, London, HMSO.

Gibson, P., Edmunds, L., Haslam, D.W. and Poskitt, E. (2002) *An Approach to Weight Management in Children and Adolescents (2-18 years) in Primary Care*, London, Royal College of Paediatrics and Child Health and National Obesity Forum.

Gregory, J., Lowe, S., Bates, C., Prentice, A., Jackson, L.V., Smithers, G., Wenlock, R. and Farron, M. (2000) *The National Diet and Nutrition Survey: Young People aged 4-18 years Vol.1 Report of the Diet and Nutrition Survey*, London, ONS/FSA/DoH.

Grogan, S. and Wainwright, N. (1996) Growing up in the Culture of Slenderness. Girls' Experiences of Body Dissatisfaction, *Women's Studies International Forum, Vol 19*, (vi) 665-673.

Haggiag, T. (2000) The Broken Jaw: A Child's Perspective. In Lask, B. and Bryant-Waugh, R. 2000 *Anorexia Nervosa and Related Eating Disorders in Childhood and Adolescence, 2nd edn*, Hove, Psychology Press Ltd.

Harris, G. and Booth, I.W. (1992) The Nature and Management of Eating Problems in Preschool Children. In Cooper, A. and Stein, A. 1992 *Feeding Problems and Eating Disorders in Children and Adolescents*, Reading, Harwood.

Helland, I.B., Smith, L., Saarem, K., Saugstad, O.D and Drevon, C.A. (2003) Maternal Supplementation with Very Long-Chain n-3 Fatty Acids during Pregnancy and Lactation Augments Children's IQ at 4 years of Age, *Pediatrics, Vol 111*, (i) e39-44.

Herman, P. and Polivy, J. (1991) Fat is a Psychological Issue, *New Scientis*t, No.1795, 41-45, Nov.16th.

Hill, A.J. (2002) Nutrition Behaviour Group Symposium on 'Evolving Attitudes to Food and Nutrition'. Developmental Issues in Attitudes to Food and Diet, *Proceedings of the Nutrition Society, Vol 61*, 259-266.

Hill, A.J., Draper, E. and Stack, J. (1994) A Weight on Children's Minds: Body Shape Dissatisfactions at 9 years old, *International Journal of Obesity, Vol 18*, 383-389.

Hill, A.J., Jones, E. and Stack, J. (1992b) A Weight on Children's Minds: Body Shape Dissatisfaction at 9 Years Old, Paper presented at the *Annual Conference of the British Psychological Society*, Scarborough, April 10th.

Hill, A.J., Oliver, S.and Rogers, P. (1992a) Eating in the Adult World: The Rise of Dieting in Childhood and Adolescence, *British Journal of Clinical Psychology. Vol 31*, 95-105.

Hill, A.J. and Robinson, A. (1991) Dieting Concerns have a Functional Effect on the Behaviour of Nine-Year Old Girls, *British Journal of Clinical Psychology, Vol 30*, 265-267.

Hill, A.J. and Silver, E.K. (1995) Fat, Friendless and Unhealthy: 9 Year Old Children's Perception of Body Shape Stereotypes, *International Journal of Obesity, Vol 19*, 423-430.

Hill, A.J., Weaver, C. and Blundell, J.E. (1990) Dieting Concerns of 10-Year-Old Girls and their Mothers, *British Journal of Clinical Psychology, Vol 29*, 346-348.

H.M. Treasury (2003) *Every Child Matters*, London, The Stationary Office.

House of Commons Health Committee (2004) *Obesity. Third Report of Session 2003-2004. Volume 1. Report, Together with Formal Minutes*, London, The Stationery Office.

Jefferson, A. and Cowbrough, K. (2004) *School Lunchbox Survey 2004*, London, Community Nutrition Group/Food Standards Agency.

Jeffrey, A.N., Voss, B.S., Metcalf, B.S., Alba, S. and Wilkin, T.J. (2005) Parents' Awareness of Overweight in Themselves and Their Children: Cross Sectional Study within a Cohort (Early Bird 21), *BMJ*, Vol 330, 23-24.

Johnson, S. and Birch, L.L. (1994) Parents' and Children's Adiposity and Eating Style, *Pediatrics, Vol 94*, (v) 653-661.

Kearney-Cooke, A. and Steichen-Asch, P. (1990) Men, Body Image, and Eating Disorders. In Anderson A.E. (ed) 1990 *Males with Eating Disorders*, Bruner/Mazel Inc., New York.

Kilbourne, J. (1994) Still Killing Us Softly: Advertising and The Obsession With Thinness. In Fallon, P., Katzman, M.A. and Wooley, S.C. (eds) 1994 *Feminist Perspectives on Eating Disorders*, The Guildford Press, New York.

Kotani, K., Nishida, M., Yamashita, S., Funahashi, T., Fujioka, S., Tokunaga, K., et al. (1997) Two Decades of Annual Medical Examinations in Japanese Obese Children: Do Obese Children Grow into Obese Adults? *International Journal of Obesity and Related Metabolic Disease, Vol 21*, 912 921.

Krebs-Smith, S.M., Heimendinger, J., Patterson, B.H., Subar, A.F., Kessler, R., Pivonka, E. (1995) Psychosocial factors associated with fruit and vegetable consumption. *American Journal of Health Promotion.* 10 (2) 98-104.

Landman, J. and Cruickshank, J. (2001) A Review of Ethnicity, Health and Nutrition-Related Diseases in Relation to Migration in the United Kingdom, *Public Health Nutrition, Vol 4*, Special Issue 2B, 647-657.

Levine, M. (1987) *How Schools Can Help Combat Student Eating Disorders: Anorexia and Bulimia* National Education Association of the United States, Washington DC.

Lister-Sharp, D., Chapman, S., Stewart-Brown, S. and Sowden, A. (1999) Health Promoting Schools and Health Promotion in Schools: Two Systematic Reviews. *Health Technology Assessment, Vol 3*, (xxii).

Lund, B.K., Gregson, K., Neale, R.J. and Tilston, C.H. (1990) The Dietary Awareness of Children: Specific Food Components, *British Food Journal, Vol 92*, (viii) 23-27.

Macintyre, S. and West, P. (1991) Social Development and Health Correlates of "Attractiveness" in Adolescence. *Sociology of Health and Illness, Vol 13*, (ii) 149-167.

Malina, R.M. and Bouchard, C. (1991) *Growth, Maturation and Physical Activity*, Leeds, Human Kinetics Publishers (UK) Ltd.

Mauthner, M., Mayall, B. and Turner, S. (1993) *Children and Food at Primary School*, Social Science

Research Unit, Institute of Education, London.

McKenzie, S. (2003) Selling Candy to a Baby, *Public Health News*, 11 August, 10-12.

Noble, C., Corney, M., Eves, A., Kipps, M. and Lumbers, M. (2001) School Meals: Primary Schoolchildren's Perceptions of the Healthiness of Foods Served at School and their Preferences for these Foods, *Health Education Journal, Vol 60*, (ii) 102-119.

O'Dea, J.A. (2005) School-Based Health Education Strategies for the Improvement of Body Image and Prevention of Eating Problems, *Health Education, Vol 105*, (i) 11-33.

OPCS (1994) *Children's Dental Health in the United Kingdom*, London, The Stationery Office.

Ottley, C. (1997) Childhood Activity and Diet in Prevention of Obesity: A Review of the Evidence, *Health Education Journal, Vol 56*, (iii) 313-320.

Patton, G.C., Selzer, R., Coffey, C., Carlin, J.B. and Wolfe, R. (1999) Onset of Adolescent Eating Disorders: Population Based Cohort Study over 3 years, *British Medical Journal, Vol 318*, (7186) 765-768.

Paterson, A. (2002) *Diet of Despair. A Book about Eating Disorders for Young People and their Families*, Bristol, Lucky Duck Publishing Ltd.

Prior, G., Deverill, C., Malbut, K. and Primatesta, P. (2003) *Health Survey for England 2001*, London, The Stationery Office.

Power, C., Lake, J.K. and Cole, T.J. (1997) Measurement and Long-Term Health Risks of Child and Adolescent Fatness. *International Journal of Obesity and Related Metabolic Disorders, Vol 21*, (vii) 507-526.

Renck Jalongo, M. (1999) Matters of Size: Obesity as a Diversity Issue in the Field of Early Childhood, *Early Childhood Education Journal, Vol 27*, (ii) 95-103.

Robinson, S. (1999) *Children's Perceptions of Eating and Body Image*, Unpublished Phd thesis, University of Southampton.

Robinson, S. (2000) Children's Perceptions of Who Controls their Food, *Journal of Human Nutrition and Dietetics, Vol 13*, 163-171.

Ross, S. (1995) "Do I Really Have to Eat That?" A Qualitative Study of School Children's Food Choices and Preferences, *Health Education Journal. Vol 54*, (iii) 312-321.

SACN (2003) *Salt and Health*, London, The Stationery Office.

Sinclair, D. (1989) *Human Growth after Birth*, 5th edition, Oxford University Press, Oxford.

Storey, P., Candappa, M. and Goodrich, R. (2005) Food for Thought. *Public Health News*, 7th February, 12-13.

Sustain (2001) *TV Dinners. What's Being Served Up By The Advertisers?* London, Sustain: The alliance for better food and farming.

Tate, A. (2000) Schooling. In Lask, B. and Bryant-Waugh, R. 2000 *Anorexia Nervosa and Related Eating Disorders in Childhood and Adolescence*, 2nd edn, Hove, Psychology Press Ltd.

The Food Commission (1994) Selling Food to Kids, *The Food Magazine, Issue 27*, 14-15.

Tilston, C.H., Gregson, K., Neale, R.J. and Douglas, C.J. (1993) Dietary Awareness of Primary School Children, *British Food Journal, Vol 93*, (vi) 25-29.

Turner, S. (1993) What do Young People Learn about Good Food and Nutrition in Schools. In Buttriss J., Hyman K. (eds) 1993 *Making Sense of Food: Children in Focus*, Proceedings of a Conference held on October 28th, National Dairy Council, London, 27-46.

Wardle, J., Volz, C. and Golding, C. (1995) Social Variation in Attitudes to Obesity in Children, *International Journal of Obesity. Vol 19*, 562-569.

Wardle, J. and Huon, G. (2000) An Experimental Investigation of The Influence of Health Information on Children's Taste Preferences. *Health Education Research, Vol 15*, (i) 39-44.

Wardle, J. (1991) Body Image and Eating Behaviour in Young People. In Health Promotion Trust 1991 *Young People: Behaviour and Opportunities*, Cambridge, Health Promotion Trust.

Watkins, B. and Lask, B. (2002) Eating Disorders in School-Aged Children, *Child and Adolescent Psychiatric Clinics of North America, Vol 11*, 185-199.

Watson, J.M. (1993) Male Body Image and Health Beliefs: A Qualitative Study and Implications for Health Promotion Practice, *Health Education Journal, Vol 52*, (iv) 246-252.

Watt, R.G., Sheiham A. (1997) Towards an Understanding of Young People's Conceptualisation of Food and Eating, *Health Education Journal, Vol 56*, (iv) 340-349.

Weber Cullen, K., Baranowski, T., Owens, E., de Moor, C., Rittenberry, L., Olvera, N. and Resnicow, K. (2002) Ethnic Differences in Social Correlates of Diet, *Health Education Research, 17*, (i) 7-18.

Wetton, N. (1986) Education in Health. Issues for The Early Years of School, *Health Education Journal, Vol 45*, (i) 28-29.

White, D. (1983) Body Salience, Weight – Role Knowledge – Flexibility and Peer Affiliation between the Ages of Three and Eight Years, Paper presented at the *Biennial Meeting of the Society for Research in Child Development*, Detroit, MI, April 21st-24th.

Whiting, M. and Lobstein, T. (1995) *Healthy Eating for Babies and Children*, London, Hodder & Stoughton.

Williams, T., Wetton, N. and Moon, A. (1989) *A Picture of Health*, London Health Education Authority.

Wynne, A. (ed) (1999) *Obesity. The Report of the British Nutrition Foundation Task Force.* Blackwell Science.

World Health Organization (1990) *WHO Technical Report Series 797: Diet, Nutrition and the Prevention of Chronic Diseases*, Geneva, WHO.

World Health Organization Europe (2006) *European Guideline for Children and Young People (7-18 years)*, Copenhagen, WHO (in press).

Appendix 1

Healthy Eating in Primary Schools: The Interviewees

Helen Brown is a Breakfast Club coordinator at the East Kent Coastal Teaching Primary Care Trust

Cherie Morgan is the Kent facilitator for The School Milk Project

Gill Aitken is a Healthy Schools coordinator at Selsted Church of England Primary School, Dover

Carmen Flynn is a Healthy Schools coordinator at Dame Janet Junior School, Ramsgate

Carol Manton is a family liaison officer at Aylcliffe Primary School, Dover

Chris Ford is a reception teacher who runs the Green Club at East Church of England School, Sheerness.

Paul Boyce is the community garden manager of the Garden Gate project and horticulture tutor at Stone Bay School, Broadstairs.

Mark Sleep is the Client Services Manager at Kent County Council. He is responsible for school meals, buildings, cleaning and window cleaning contracts, and the catering adviser for the Education department.

Jill Flavin is the Healthy Schools coordinator at Shatterlocks Infant School, Dover.

Mog Marchant is the catering manager at Northfleet School for Girls.

Georgina Ayin is a nutrition consultant who coordinates the Kent Heartbeat Award Scheme.

Gillian Trumble is an advanced skills teacher in Citizenship at Chatham House Grammar School.

Sharon Bremner is a Healthy Schools coordinator at St Radigunds Primary School, Dover.

Kerry Collins is a family liaison officer and a healthy schools coordinator at Mongeham Primary School, Deal.

Jackie Moull is a family liaison officer at Linden Grove School, Ashford.

Brian Molloy M.B.E. is the director of the Schools' Counselling Service in East Kent.

Chris Beer is the school nurse team leader for East Kent Community Primary Care Trust.

Fiona Annis, school nurse team leader, East Kent Community Primary Care Trust.

Carol Boxall is the school nurse (adolescent lead) for East Kent Community Primary Care Trust.

Dr Liz Tanner is a community paediatrician for Canterbury Coastal Primary Care Trust.

Jennifer Holland is the coordinator for the East Kent Healthy Schools Scheme.

Paula Gill is a community networker at Project Sunlight, a Healthy Living Network for Medway.

Carla Maurici is a registered nutritionist working for one of the leading suppliers of school meals in the UK.

Camilla Joarder is the senior dental officer for dental health promotion for the East Kent Community Dental Service, employed by Ashford Primary Care Trust.

Sue Scrivens is a dental therapist working across Kent.

Abi Mogridge is the head of community dietetics for East Kent.

Appendix 2

Useful Information: Organisations and Websites

5 A Day Programme

www.5ADAY.nhs.uk

ADHD

NICE (2000) *Guidance on the Use of Methylphenidate (Ritalin, Equasym) for Attention Deficit/Hyperactivity Disorder (ADHD) in Childhood*
www.nice.org.uk/article.asp?a=11667

Allergy UK

No 3 White Oak Square
London Road
Swanley,
Kent
BR8 7AG

www.allergyuk.org

Antidote: Campaign for Emotional Literacy

Cityside House
3rd Floor (c/o Happy Computers)
40 Adler Street
London
E1 1EE
Tel. 020 7247 3355

www.antidote.org.uk

Association for the Study of Obesity

ASO Administrative Officer
20 Brook Meadow Close
Woodford Green
Essex
IG8 9NR

www.aso.org.uk

Breakfast Club Plus

www.breakfast-club.co.uk

British Association for Counselling and Psychotherapy

BACP House
35-37 Albert Street
Rugby

Warwickshire
CV21 2SG
Tel. 0870 443 5252

www.bacp.co.uk

British Association of Dental Therapists

Tel. 0118 947 9399

www.badt.org.uk

British Dental Association

BDA mouth www.3dmouth.org

British Dental Health Foundation

Smile House
2 East Union Street
Rugby
Warwickshire
CV22 6AJ
Tel. 0870 770 4014

www.dentalhealth.org.uk

British Dietetic Association

5th Floor
Charles House
148/9 Great Charles Street
Queensway
Birmingham
B3 3HT
Tel. 0121 200 8080

www.bda.uk.com

British Heart Foundation

14 Fitzhardinge Street
London
W1H 6DH
Tel. 020 7935 0185

www.bhf.org.uk

British Nutrition Foundation

High Holborn House
52-54 High Holborn
London
WC1V 6RQ
Tel. 020 7404 6504

www.nutrition.org.uk

British Sandwich Association

www.sandwich.org.uk/Recipies.asp

Cereal Offenders (Consumers' Association)

www.which.net/campaigns/food/nutrition/0403cerealoffenders.pdf

ChildLine

www.childline.org.uk

ChildLine's web site about children's eating problems www.childline.org.uk/eatingproblems.asp

Children and Families Directorate

www.dfes.gov.uk/childrenandfamilies

Children First for Health

www.childrenfirst.nhs.uk

Children's and Young People's Unit

www.cypu.gov.uk/corporate/index.cfm

Children's Services

www.dh.gov.uk/PolicyAndGuidance/HealthAndSocialCareTopics/ChildrenServices/fs/en

Colgate–Palmolive (UK) Ltd

Guildford Business Park
Middleton Road
Guildford
Surrey
GU2 8JZ

www.colgate.co.uk

Cook Club

www.nutition.org.uk/cookclub

Cool Meals

www.coolmeals.co.uk

Drinking Water Inspectorate

55 Whitehall
London
SW1A 2EY

www.dwi.gov.uk

Eating Disorders Association

103 Prince of Wales Road
Norwich
NR1 1DW
Tel. 0870 770 3256

www.edauk.org/aboutus/index.asp

Eco Schools

www.eco-schools.org.uk

Eco Schools (England)

ENCAMS
Elizabeth House
The Pier
Wigan
WN3 4EX

Eco-Schools (Northern Ireland)

Tidy Northern Ireland
1st Floor, Studio A
89 Holywood Road
Belfast
BT4 3BA

Eco-Schools (Scotland)

Keep Scotland Beautiful
Islay House
Livilands Lane
Stirling
FK8 2BG

Eco-Schools (Wales)

Keep Wales Tidy Campaign
33/35 Cathedral Road
Cardiff
CF11 9HB

Eco-Schools Newsletters

www.eco-schools.org/new/newsletters.htm

Feed Me Better Campaign (Jamie Oliver)

www.feedmebetter.com

Focus on Food

Waitrose
South Industrial Area
Bracknel
Berkshire
RG12 8YA
Tel. 01344 824114

www.waitrose.com/focusonfood.asp

Food Dudes

www.fooddudes.co.uk

Food Standards Agency

Aviation House
125 Kingsway
London
WC2B 6NH

Tel. 020 7276 8000

www.food.gov.uk

Fruit Tuck Shops in Primary Schools (Wales)

www.food.gov.uk/multimedia/pdfs/fruittuckwales.pdf

Grab 5

www.sustainweb.org/grab5_index.asp

Growing Schools

www.teachernet.gov.uk/growingschools

Health Education Trust

18 High Street
Broom
Alcester
Warwickshire
B50 4HJ

www.healthedtrust.com

Healthier Lunch Box (tips)

www.food.gov.uk/news/newsarchive/toplunchboxtips

Kent Healthy Schools

www.kenthealthyschools.org

Kent Heartbeat Award

www.kenthealthyschools.org/healthyeating.html

Local Food Works

www.localfoodworks.org

Milk Development Council

Stroud Road
Cirencester
GL7 6JN
Tel. 01285 646500

www.mdc.co.uk

National Centre for Eating Disorders

54 New Road
Esher
Surrey
KT10 9NU
Tel. 01372 469493

www.eating-disorders.org.uk

National Centre for Eating Disorders

54 New Road
Esher
Surrey
KT10 9NU
Tel. 01372 469493

www.eating-disorders.org.uk

National Institute of Clinical Excellence (NICE)

MidCity Place
High Holborn
London
WC1V 6NA

www.nice.org.uk

National Osteoporosis Society

Camerton
Bath
BA2 OPJ
Tel. 01761 471771

www.nos.org.uk

Oral B

Gillette Group UK Ltd
Gillette Corner
Great West Road
Isleworth
Middlesex TW7 5NP
Tel. 020 83268862

Oral B Teaching Tools

www.oralb.com/learningcenter

School Fruit and Vegetable Scheme

www.5ADAY.nhs.uk

School Lunch Box Survey 2003

www.food.gov.uk/multimedia/pdfs/lunchsurvey.pdf

School Nurse Practice Development Resource Pack

www.publications.doh.gov.uk/cno/schoolnursedevpack.pdf

School Nutrition Action Groups

www.healthedtrust.com/pages/snag.htm

Schools Councils UK

Resources Department
57 Etchingham Park Road
London
N3 2EB
Tel. 020 8349 1917

www.schoolcouncils.org

Social Emotional and Behavioural Difficulties Association (SEBDA)

c/o Ted Cole
SEBDA Head Office
Church House
1 St Andrew's View
Penrith
Cumbria
CA10 7YF
Tel. 01768 210510

www.awcebd.co.uk

Soil Association

Bristol House
40-56 Victoria Street

Bristol
BS1 6BY
Tel. 0117 314 5000

www.soilassociation.org

SUSTAIN

94 White Lion Street
London
N1 9PF
Tel. 020 7837 1228

www.sustainweb.org

The Beginners Guide to Growing Vegetables

www.thebeginnersguidetogrowingvegetables.co.uk

The Caroline Walker Trust

PO Box 61
St Austell
PL26 6YL
Tel: 01726 844107

www.cwt.org.uk

The Colgate Kids

www.colgate.co.uk/oralcare/index.shtml

The Dairy Council

164 Shaftesbury Avenue
London
WC2H 8HL
Tel. 020 739 54030

www.milk.co.uk

The Food Commission

94 White Lion Street
London
N1 9PF

www.foodcomm.org.uk

The Free Fruit Initiative (Scotland)

www.scotland.gov.uk/Topics/Education/School-Education/18922/15774

The Mental Health Foundation

7th Floor
83 Victoria Street
London

SW1H 0HW
Tel. 020 7802 0300

www.mentalhealth.org.uk

The Nutrition Department

Initial Catering Services Ltd
Bridge House
Mathisen Way
Colnbrook
Berkshire
SL3 0HH
Tel: 01753 561730

The Nutrition Society

10 Cambridge Court
210 Shepherds Bush Road
London
W6 7N7

www.nutritionsociety.org.uk

The Obesity Awareness and Solutions Trust (TOAST)

PO Box 6430
Harlow
Essex
CM18 7TT
Tel. 01279 866010

www.toast-uk.org.uk

The School Milk Project

www.schoolmilk.co.uk

Thrive

The Society for Horticultural Therapy Charity
The Geoffrey Udall Centre
Beech Hill
Reading
RG7 2AT
Tel. 0118 988 5688

www.thrive.org.uk

Water Education

www.scottishwater.co.uk/education

www.3valleys.co.uk/education/index.shtml

Water is Cool in School Campaign

c/o Enuresis Resource and Information Centre
34 Old School House
Britannia Road
Kingswood
Bristol
BS15 8DB
Tel. 0117 960 3060

www.wateriscoolinschool.org.uk

Water UK

1 Queen Anne's Gate
London
SW1H 9BT
Tel. 020 7344 1866

www.water.org.uk/waterforhealth

Wired for Health

www.wiredforhealth.gov.uk

Appendix 3

Useful Books

Bradshaw, J. (ed) (2002) *The Wellbeing of Children in the UK*, London, Save the Children ISBN 1841870609.

British Nutrition Foundation (2002) *Nutrition, Health and Schoolchildren*, London, BNF.

Department of Health (2005) *Choosing a Better Diet. A Food and Health Action Plan*, London, Department of Health. Available directly from Department of Health, PO Box 777, London SE1 6XH Telephone 08701 555455.

Dowler, E., Turner, S. and Dobson, B. (2001) *Poverty bites: Food, Health and Poor Families*, London, Child Poverty Action Group ISBN 1901698459.

Lask, B. and Bryant-Waugh, R. (eds) (2000) *Anorexia Nervosa and Related Eating Disorders in Childhood and Adolescence*, Hove, Psychological Press Ltd. ISBN 0863778038.

Sullivan, K. (2004) *How to help your Overweight Child... eat healthily and well, enjoy exercise, boost self-esteem and self respect, achieve a healthier weight*, London, Rodale Int.Ltd. ISBN 1405077328.